Working in the
Voluntary
Sector

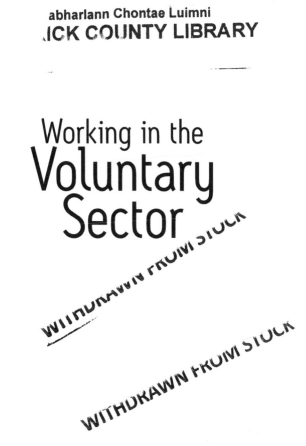

If you want to know how...

Planning Your Gap Year
*Hundreds of opportunities for employment, study,
volunteer work and independent travel*

'A magnificent tool.' – *The Guardian*

'Practical advice on planning, how to utilise the internet for
preparation and details of more than 220 organisations
worldwide.' – *Evening Standard*

Worldwide Volunteering
*Hundreds of volunteer organisations for
gap year, holiday or vacation projects*

'The book demonstrates the enormous range of
opportunities that exist around the world.
There is something for everyone.' – *Richard Branson*

'If you do not already have this book on your career library
shelves, invest in a copy now.' – *Phoenix*

howtobooks

Please send for a free copy of the latest catalogue:

How To Books
3 Newtec Place, Magdalen Road,
Oxford OX4 1RE, United Kingdom
email: info@howtobooks.co.uk
http://www.howtobooks.co.uk

Working in the
Voluntary
Sector

REVISED AND UPDATED · FOURTH EDITION · **4**TH

CRAIG BROWN

howtobooks

Published by How To Books Ltd,
3 Newtec Place, Magdalen Road,
Oxford OX4 1RE. United Kingdom.
Tel: (01865) 793806. Fax: (01865) 248780.
email: info@howtobooks.co.uk
http://www.howtobooks.co.uk

First edition 1998
Second edition 2001
Third edition 2002
Fourth edition 2005

British Library Cataloguing in Publication Data
A catalogue record for this book is available from the British
Library

Cover design by Baseline Arts Ltd, Oxford
Produced for How To Books by Deer Park Productions
Typeset by PDQ Typesetting, Newcastle-under-Lyme, Staffs.
Printed and bound by The Cromwell Press, Trowbridge,
Wiltshire

NOTE: The material contained in this book is set out in good
faith for general guidance and no liability can be accepted
for loss or expense incurred as a result of relying in particular
circumstances on statements made in the book. The laws and
regulations are complex and liable to change, and readers should
check the current position with the relevant authorities before
making personal arrangements.

Contents

List of Illustrations

Preface

Many people have had some contact with the voluntary sector through volunteering, but it is also worth considering the sector as a viable option for career development. It is increasing in size and importance and can offer the chance to develop all of the skills that have usually been thought of as the preserve of the private sector. What makes the voluntary sector more attractive, perhaps, than the private sector is the traditional value it places on people as individuals. Business skills, interpersonal skills and respect for individuals go hand in hand in the voluntary sector.

This book shows that working in the voluntary sector – as a volunteer or as a paid member of staff – can be rewarding in terms of your career, your personal development and your enjoyment. It explains how the voluntary sector works, how to find work, and how to develop your career (or just get real job satisfaction) by working as a volunteer or paid worker. Whether you are starting out from college, returning to work or even working in the private sector and looking for ways to enhance your skills, this book will help you to find the right opportunities.

Thank you to those who helped me: Sue, for her patience, reading drafts, suggesting amendments and challenging my assumptions (and typing out most of the addresses in Chapters 9 and 10); Kathryn, for reading drafts and suggesting amendments; Environ, Greenpeace, Lambeth Shad, The National Autistic Society, Virginia House Settlement and The Winged Fellowship Trust for permission to reproduce their materials; private and public sector employers (from McDonalds to the NHS) for responding to my questionnaire; and all those people who inspired (and sometimes appear in) the case studies.

Craig Brown

Understanding the Voluntary Sector

COMPARING CHARITIES AND VOLUNTARY BODIES

The voluntary sector is huge and incredibly diverse. Opportunities for rewarding work, both paid and unpaid, are abundant.

The more you know about the voluntary sector and the organisations in it the easier it will be for you to decide if you really want to work in it. You'll also be clearer about the kind of work you want to do and you'll understand how to go about getting it.

Broadly speaking there are two types of organisation in the voluntary sector:

1. charities
2. non-charitable voluntary bodies.

In this book they are both referred to as voluntary sector organisations. They work in almost every area of life at local, national and international levels.

Recognising a charity

Each year around 12,000 new charities are added to the Charity Register and around 10,000 are removed. At the moment there are close to 200,000 charities in the UK although about 30,000 of these are subsidiaries or branches of others. For example, every branch of Relate is registered as an individual charity, though they are part of the main organisation.

An organisation can only be a charity if it works in the public interest and not just to further the interests of certain individuals. It must do one or more of the following:

◆ relieve poverty, disability and/or distress
◆ advance education
◆ advance religion
◆ do other charitable things that benefit the community.

The last condition is a catchall; so, for example, animal rescue organisations come under this category.

There are tight restrictions on the kind of activities charities can get involved in and the way they are run. For example, they can't promote political views, which is why organisations like Amnesty International, which is often very critical of governments, cannot be charities. Also, the people who have overall legal responsibility for running charities – the trustees – are not allowed to receive any financial rewards for their work.

The Charity Commission for England and Wales produces a booklet called *Registering as a Charity*. It's aimed at people who want to set up their own organisation, but it's also a very useful introduction to understanding charities.

Recognising a voluntary body

There are as many voluntary bodies in the UK as there are charities – around 200,000. They range from your local amateur football team or hill-walking group, to internationally known organisations like Greenpeace and Amnesty International.

The definition of a voluntary body is that it uses volunteers for some of its activities and that it is non-profitable. There could be a number of reasons why such a body does not become a charity:

- it might not meet any of the conditions for being a charity
- it could be involved in political activities
- the people running it might not be ready to apply to be a charity
- it might be a public body (like the Special Constabulary).

UNDERSTANDING HOW CHARITIES AND VOLUNTARY BODIES WORK

In many ways working in the voluntary sector is similar to working in any other type of environment, though there are some important differences.

Raising money

Like any business, voluntary sector organisations need money. However, they don't have shareholders and therefore the reason they need money is not to make profits for the sake of profit, but to continue doing the work they were set up to do. They can raise money in a number of ways:

- through grants from public (government/local authority) funds
- by fundraising
- from membership fees
- by selling goods and/or services.

Needing skills

Raising money, administering it, providing services and achieving the aims of the organisation all require skills as sound as you would find in the commercial world. Just as in business, voluntary sector organisations need to make use of real, solid work skills in order to function properly – skills in areas such as:

- administration
- finance
- marketing
- fundraising
- publicity
- research
- information technology
- specialist skills according to the nature of the organisation, e.g. medical, agricultural, technical, scientific and so on.

Responding to customers

In the voluntary sector customers are often referred to as clients and they are the people who benefit from what the organisations do. For example, homeless people are clients of organisations like Shelter.

If you work in the voluntary sector you may very soon hear two phrases: 'needs led' and 'funding led'. They refer to the way an organisation decides its priorities and can be the subject of fierce debate between the service providers and the fundraisers in an organisation.

'Funding led' means that decisions on policy and work areas are taken on the basis of what the money can be raised for. But 'needs led' means that priorities are decided according to the needs of the clients, whether or not they are easy to raise money for.

Some causes are easier to raise money for than others, even though they may be equally deserving. Children are easy to raise money for – the Children in Need television appeal raises enough money in one day to put it in the top ten charitable trusts. However, mental health is a notoriously difficult cause to raise funds for.

Committing to equal opportunities

Voluntary sector organisations are usually very committed to equal opportunities. This affects their policies on recruitment, as well as promotion, pay, and terms and conditions. One advantage of this should be that everyone knows where they stand, what the rewards are and how they work.

Another advantage should be that the recruitment information and process really is fair and designed to recruit the best person for the job regardless of age, gender, race, ethnic background, religion, disability, sexual orientation, family background or social status.

Often the results are impressive and better than those of many private sector organisations. This isn't just about equal opportunities, but about a very real concern to get the best person for the job and use limited resources as effectively as possible.

You might sometimes read statements on job adverts encouraging applications from ethnic minorities and/or people with disabilities. In fact some work may be open only to particular groups because the nature of the work being done means it is excluded from the provisions of the Race, Sex or Disability Discrimination Acts.

Being positive

Some organisations have client groups who are disadvantaged not only by their situation, but by the way other people perceive them. One way of helping such clients is to challenge those perceptions by changing the way we describe people or things.

This has made the voluntary sector something of a champion of 'political correctness', which is essentially about valuing people, not being judgmental and avoiding stereotypes.

A good example of positive political correctness is the Spastics Society changing its name to Scope (for People with Cerebral Palsy). The word 'spastic' had grown to be used as an insult and it devalued the people who suffered from cerebral palsy. By changing the organisation's name the perception of its client group also changes. Another word for 'scope' is 'potential', which is positive, and using the phrase 'people with cerebral palsy' puts people before the condition and emphasises the human connection between those of us who do not suffer from it and those who do.

Volunteering

A volunteer is someone who gives their time freely without expecting a financial reward. This means that they are often very committed and work extremely hard. However, because they do not have to do it and so can stop at any time, volunteers need to be motivated and managed in ways that are different from paid workers. In most cases a volunteer cannot be told to do something, they can only be asked.

Many voluntary sector organisations rely heavily on the volunteer help they get. The volunteers in turn become 'stakeholders' in the organisation. In other words they have a concern for how the organisation is run and for its future. Some organisations address this by developing membership schemes for volunteers that give them voting rights at annual meetings. This leads to a greater feeling of ownership of the organisation for the volunteers and a real sense of having a say in the way things are done.

Managing

Committees usually run voluntary sector organisations. In charities these are called boards of trustees or management committees and they have legal obligations and restrictions to observe. Voluntary bodies may have similar committees or they may just have a loose collection of people who 'run the show'.

The committee may meet from once a year to once a week depending on its role, its obligations, and the size and nature of the organisation it is responsible for. Some committees have a very hands-off approach and meet only for progress updates on how the organisation is meeting its objectives. Other committees may be more active with individuals meeting employees and volunteers, producing discussion documents and taking a real and immediate interest in the day-to-day work.

One point to bear in mind about working in an organisation run by a committee is that major policy decisions need its blessing, so when a committee meets only once every four months this can slow down the pace of change. While this can mean that there is more time for reflection on the suitability of any action, on the other hand it can be very frustrating.

FUNDRAISING AND ITS IMPORTANCE

Fundraising is probably the most common way for most people to come into contact with a voluntary sector organisation. Children come home from school with forms for sponsored swims, the local church holds a jumble sale, there are fundraising telethons and concerts, and of course people in the street with collection tins.

Fundraising does two jobs for voluntary sector organisa-tions:

1. it raises money
2. it raises awareness.

Both are very important because they affect the stability of the organisation and the effectiveness of its work. If you are finding out about an organisation or you have got as far as the interview stage for a job, it is a good idea to find out how it gets its money.

There are lots of different ways for an organisation to raise money:

- Applying for grants from local, national or international government bodies.

- Applying for grants from trusts (trusts are charities that give money to specific causes).

- Encouraging donations from companies by, for example, sponsorship deals.

- Encouraging donations from individuals through street collections, mailshots, TV appeals and so on.

- Getting donations from support groups that might, for example, organise jumble sales or sponsored walks.

- Getting income from membership fees, in return for which members get regular updates about the organisation's work.

- Selling products (through catalogues and shops) or services (such as consultancy work).

Effective fundraising is a highly skilled job. Individuals tend to give to what they can relate to or to things which have a strong emotional pull. But businesses, trusts and governments have strict rules and guidelines about how they allocate funds and organisations have to show how they match up. The competition for funds is intense, so skilled fundraisers are highly valued.

If you are applying to a small voluntary sector organisation for paid work and you are concerned about job security you need to consider its track record in fundraising.

LOOKING AT OPPORTUNITIES FOR WORK

Because the sector is so large and diverse, then whatever your skills and interests there will be something you can do either in a voluntary capacity or as a paid worker. Here's a small list – and it is very small – of the kind of work you could do:

advising	gardening	rescuing
befriending	guiding	researching
building	informing	restoring
campaigning	leading	retailing
computing	lobbying	surveying
cooking	managing	training
counselling	nursing	treating
driving	performing	writing

Organisations vary in size, from those run by only one or two people, to those with hundreds of employees. There are lots of small local organisations and many of the larger ones operate at local levels, so there should be something available close to where you live. On the other hand, if you want a paid position at the heart of a major organisation you need to remember that the majority are based in and around London.

FINDING OUT MORE

The first thing to do is get the contact details for the organisation you are interested in. You'll need a name, a telephone number and an address. If you don't have a contact name then 'the personnel department' or 'the volunteer co-ordinator' will do, depending on whether you are looking for paid or voluntary work.

There are lots of organisations listed in Chapters 9 and 10 of this book. You can also try telephone directories, *The Voluntary Agencies Directory* and financial profile directories such as Baring Asset Management *Top 3,000 Charities*, all of which should be available in major reference libraries. If the organisation is local you should be able to find out about it from your nearest volunteer bureau.

Some questions to ask

If you manage to speak to someone at the head office of an organisation, it will be useful to be clear about the information you want. Have a pad and pen to hand so you can jot down some notes.

- ◆ What does the organisation do – activities, when, where?

- ◆ Where is it based or run from?

- ◆ How many staff and volunteers does it have?

- ◆ Who benefits from the work they do?

- ◆ How do they do their fundraising and how financially healthy are they?

- ◆ (If you want a paid position) does it ever have any paid positions available and how can you find out about them?

◆ (If you want to volunteer) what kind of help do they need?

◆ Can you go and visit them or one of their projects to find out more? (They may not encourage this, but there's no harm in asking.)

◆ Can they send you some information – general information/publicity, annual review, corporate strategy and anything else they are able to let you have?

If you are writing for information it is better to send loose stamps than an SAE, unless you know what size of envelope the information will need.

Reading up on the voluntary sector
A lot of texts about the voluntary sector are quite dry and academic, but it is probably worth exploring the library to see if there is anything that interests you.

One book worth reading is *Understanding Voluntary Organisations* by Charles Handy (published by Penguin). It's especially useful if you are interested in working in administration or management in the voluntary sector. Also, the voluntary sector has its own magazine, *Third Sector*, which you may be able to get hold of through your local reference library (it is also available online at www.thirdsector.co.uk).

Going on courses
You can do courses to find out about work in the

voluntary sector before deciding if it's what you want. These courses are designed mainly for people wanting paid work. They range from half-day workshops to week-long seminars with work placements in a host charity.

For more information you should contact:

◆ CF Appointments Ltd, Lloyds Court, 1 Goodman's Yard, London E1 8AT. Tel: (020) 7953 1191. www.cfappointments.com
Email: enquiries@cfappointments.com

◆ Charity People, 38 Bedford Place, Bloomsbury, London WC1B 5JH. Tel: (020) 7299 8700. www.charitypeople.co.uk

◆ Working for a Charity, NCVO, Regent's Wharf, 8 All Saints Street, London N1 9RL. Tel: (020) 7520 2512. www.wfac.org.uk Email: enquiries@wfac.org.uk

Also your local volunteer bureau may know if there are any local courses available.

Some organisations that recruit a large number of volunteers may run open days, seminar evenings or workshops for potential volunteers. These events will often have volunteers on hand to answer questions, so they are well worth going along to. They are usually advertised in local newspapers. Otherwise you could contact the organisation you are interested in to see if they do anything similar.

CHECKLIST
◆ How would you define a voluntary sector organisation?

- ◆ What are the distinctive features about working in the voluntary sector?

- ◆ How are charities different from non-charitable voluntary bodies?

- ◆ Why is fundraising so important?

- ◆ What can you do to find out more about the voluntary sector?

USEFUL RESOURCES

Useful addresses

These are addresses of bodies that regulate or provide advice and other services for the voluntary sector. Addresses of individual voluntary sector organisations can be found in Chapters 9 and 10 (and, where relevant, at the end of each of the other chapters).

Charity Commission for England and Wales, Harmsworth House, 13–15 Bouverie St, London EC4Y 8DP. Tel: (0870) 333 0123. www.charity-commission.gov.uk

Directory of Social Change (DSC), 24 Stephenson Way, London NW1 2DP. Tel: (020) 7391 4800. www.dsc.org.uk E-mail: info@dsc.org.uk.

Northern Ireland Council for Voluntary Action, 61 Duncairn Gardens, Belfast BT15 2GB. Tel: 028 9087 7777. www.nicva.org E-mail:info@nicva.org

National Council for Voluntary Organisations (NCVO), Regents Wharf, 8 All Saints Street, London N1 9RL. Tel: (020) 7713 6161. www.ncvo.vol.org.uk E-mail: helpdesk@ncvo-vol.org.uk

Scottish Council for Voluntary Organisations, The Mansfield Traquair Centre, 15 Mansfield Place, Edinburgh

EH3 6BB. Tel: (0131) 556 3882. www.scvo.org.uk
E-mail: enquiries@scvo.org.uk
Wales Council for Voluntary Action (WCVA), Baltic House, Mount Stuart Square, Cardiff Bay, Cardiff CF10 5FH. Tel: 0870 6071666. www.wcva.org.uk Email: help@wcva.org.uk

(2)

Working in the Voluntary Sector

WANTING TO DO IT

There are probably as many reasons for choosing to work in the voluntary sector as there are organisations in it. Whatever your reasons are, it's important to spend some time thinking about them. Knowing why you want to do it will help you to identify the right job or voluntary work; it will also help when it comes to thinking about your strategy for getting that work. Whether you are looking for paid work, or to be a volunteer, you'll need to consider the issues in this chapter.

Believing in a cause

For many people this is an important starting point. There are a lot of people at all levels of the sector, paid and unpaid, who do what they do because they believe in the cause they are working for. 'Wanting to make a difference', or 'contributing to' or 'giving something back to' society can be a very important motivator.

If believing in a cause is part of your motivation, think about the following:

♦ How focused is your belief? The more specific you can be about what it is that you believe in, what it is that fires you up, the better your chances of finding the right job later.

◆ Can you back up what you believe in with real knowledge about the facts, the debates and the issues? The more you know about an issue the clearer you will be about what kind of organisation you would like to work for. Doing some voluntary work can be a way of finding out more, before committing yourself further.

Improving your CV

Volunteering
Working as a volunteer can look good on your CV for a number of reasons:

1. If you've had any periods of unemployment and can show that you stayed busy, doing something worthwhile, it makes the point that you don't waste your time.

2. If the people skills needed for a job don't appear in the work experience on your CV, you may be able to show that you have developed these skills through volunteering.

3. If you have only recently finished your education and so don't have much paid work experience, being able to put voluntary work on your CV could show qualities like maturity, initiative, commitment and willingness to take on responsibility.

Paid work

More and more employers are recognising that the ability to work with the pressures and tensions of the voluntary sector is transferable to the private sector with its emphasis on teams, flexibility and customer focus. On the other hand, there are still many potential employers who may think you are out of touch with the world of business and its fast pace, its deadlines and its competitiveness. This is something you will have to judge for yourself, and it may affect how long you decide to work in the voluntary sector.

Developing your career

For many people the voluntary sector is where their career is. But for others it is part of their plan to move upwards in the private sector.

Making a career in the voluntary sector

◆ Are you happy to stay in one job or do you want promotions? The size of the organisation you work for will affect your chances of promotion. You're more likely to get a promotion in a larger organisation, but you could get bigger responsibilities earlier in a small one.

◆ Is job security important to you? Causes, to some extent, come and go like fashions. Voluntary organisations relying on external funders for their income can be vulnerable to changing trends.

◆ Is money important to you? Some larger organisations pay well, but salaries for equivalent jobs in the private sector are usually much higher. (See Chapter 6 for more information on this.)

- Is the organisation you want to work for unique? If it is you could be working on 'ground-breaking' issues and the sense of personal contribution will be magnified – but will it fix you in a corner?

- Are you prepared to spend a lot of time volunteering? Being a volunteer is often a way of showing commitment to a cause and it also develops your own understanding of the issues involved.

- Once you're on the paid staff progression could mean studying for qualifications at some time, because more and more organisations are becoming more business-like in how they are run.

Making the voluntary sector part of your career plan
It could be that you want to do some paid work in the voluntary sector before moving on to the private sector. Or you might be looking for voluntary work to build up new skills that you can use in your workplace. Consider the following:

- Try to find out how your employer/future employer/ professional association regards the voluntary sector. Some see it in a positive light, especially for the people skills that can be developed. Others may see it as a soft option, or not see what relevance such work has in the business world.

- Be very clear about the kind of voluntary sector organisation you want to work for and investigate carefully whether it will provide you with the opportunities to develop the right skills.

Developing your skills, knowledge and understanding
Volunteering could be an ideal way to learn new things in your spare time.

It may be that there are certain skills you would like to develop, knowledge you would like to gain, or issues you would like to understand. For example, you might want to learn valuable skills such as conflict resolution or negotiation, so working as a volunteer with a local community mediation project could help you develop these. You might want to develop some building or gardening skills and going on regular weekend workcamps could provide you with an opportunity. You might want to work overseas to experience living in another culture.

It's important to think of skills in a very wide sense when looking at the voluntary sector in relation to your future career plans. For example, if you want to work in the emergency services, any voluntary work you have done that has brought you into contact with a wide cross-section of people will be invaluable.

Returning to work
Whether you have been out of work because you have been made redundant or have been raising a family, being a volunteer can be an ideal starting point for getting back to work. However, there are a few things to consider:

♦ Voluntary sector organisations aren't obliged to take your help – they recognise that you want to get something out of the experience for yourself, but they'll want to know that you're able to put something worthwhile back in.

- Using your free time to volunteer while you are out of work shows potential employers that you are motivated and self-disciplined – after all, you don't have to do it.

- Volunteering can get you mixing with lots of different people, increasing your confidence after a period out of work, as well as providing opportunities for networking.

- A paid placement with a voluntary sector organisation may be one of your options under the New Deal scheme. (See Chapter 4 for more information about this.)

Changing direction

Changing jobs is quite normal these days and it is not unusual for people to have three or more different careers in their lifetime. If you are considering a career change it may be worth giving your ideas a trial run before committing yourself to making such a major decision. For example, you may be thinking about going into hotel work, so you could test out how you react to and feel about a similar environment by volunteering either as a temporary Youth Hostel warden or as a worker in a refuge or homeless people's hostel. The fact that you've tried something out (even though it isn't exactly the same) will look good on your CV.

Meeting people

Volunteering can be a good way of meeting people with common interests and the same outlook on life. But you need to think carefully about the kind of volunteer activity that you are willing to do. Would it be better to be

a volunteer fundraiser for a local hospice than be a prison visitor? As a fundraiser you could get involved in lots of activities, but as a visitor you would need lots of emotional resilience.

Having time on your hands

If you are retired or nearing retirement being a volunteer can be an excellent way of staying active and maintaining a wide social circle. It can also be fulfilling to share all your years of experience with others that could benefit from it.

Having fun

Last, but by no means least, one of the main motivators in work today is enjoyment. More employers are recognising the importance of people enjoying the work they do.

Wanting job satisfaction may be a major factor in your decision to seek paid work in the voluntary sector, or you may simply be looking for something different and enjoyable to do in your spare time.

Bear in mind that while there is a great deal of job satisfaction to be had from working or volunteering in the voluntary sector, it also has its fair share of mundane jobs and you need to go into it with your eyes open.

DOING PAID OR UNPAID WORK

Getting paid work

The range of jobs

Whatever skills and qualifications you have, it is likely that there is something in the voluntary sector that you can do. The important thing to be aware of is that for paid positions a sense of commitment has to be backed up by real skills (unless, of course, it is an entry-level position with training provided). In this respect the voluntary sector is no different from the private sector.

Here are some examples of paid jobs in the voluntary sector; it is by no means an exhaustive list:

- accountant/finance assistant/personnel officer

- carer/befriender/counsellor

- child worker/community worker/rights worker

- conservation officer/ecologist/city-farm worker

- director/manager/project manager/volunteer co-ordinator

- fundraiser/campaigns officer/grants officer

- lawyer/psychologist/scientist

- mechanic/architect/carpenter

- nurse/therapist/doctor

- programmer/systems analyst/network manager

- researcher/information analyst/journalist/lobbyist

- secretary/clerk/admin assistant/receptionist

- trainer/vocational instructor/teacher.

Working full-time
Working hours are normally 35–40 hours a week, although heavy workloads, few staff and funding constraints can mean working many more hours than this.

When deadlines are tight or workloads are heavy it is normal to put in the extra hours needed and not be paid for them – many organisations operate a time-off-in-lieu (TOIL) system. However, there is always the exception and occasionally a full-time position in the voluntary sector can appear for as few as 30 hours per week and still be quite well paid.

Working part-time
There are lots of part-time positions in the voluntary sector, at all levels. There are just a few things to consider:

◆ There can be a good deal of flexibility concerning when you do your hours.

◆ Part-time work may be worth taking to get a 'foot in the door'.

◆ If you are receiving benefits, they may be affected by the hours you work and the amount of money you are paid.

Job-sharing
Job-sharing is a way of doing a full-time job, part-time. You simply share your position with another person. The most usual arrangement is to split the days or weeks in half. Not all organisations offer this kind of option and you will need to think about the following:

◆ It might be up to you to find someone to job-share with.

◆ You'll need to be able to work with the other person extremely well – you may not see them much, but you'll be working on the same things so you'll need to be very organised and co-ordinated and communicate well with each other.

Working on a permanent or temporary basis
There are many positions in the voluntary sector recruited on a permanent basis. However, many are recruited on fixed-term contracts, often due to funding constraints. It may be that you are already clear about which type of position you want, though it will be worth thinking over the following issues:

◆ Permanent work provides a measure of security and may give you access to opportunities that won't be available to temporary staff.

◆ On the other hand, a series of temporary contracts could expose you to lots of different opportunities and will certainly give you lots of contacts.

◆ Temporary work can be very exciting because it can be focused on short-term projects.

◆ Temporary work can also be very dull, made up of the easy-to-delegate and less interesting work.

◆ Short-term temporary work can be unsettling and stressful because of the insecurity – though it can also be a useful filler.

Taking secondment or leave of absence
Some employers encourage secondments or leaves of absence to do work in the voluntary sector. It may be worth approaching your manager to see if he or she would be open to the idea. You would need to be able to show

your employer not only that what you would be doing is worthwhile but also how the company would benefit from it on your return.

A leave of absence is unpaid, whereas with a secondment your employer continues to pay you for the duration.

Things to consider:

◆ How supportive is your boss/company?

◆ Will taking time out mean you miss out on some interesting work or a promotion prospect with your employer? Or will it benefit your career?

◆ Can you afford to take a leave of absence? Your employer will not be paying you and the voluntary sector organisation you are working for may not be paying you much. How long can you afford to take a leave of absence for? People taking a leave of absence to work on overseas development projects for two years often sell their houses, or rent them out.

◆ Are you willing to take the risk of not having a job to return to? During your absence your employer may make changes, which mean that you end up with a different job from the one you left, or have no job to return to.

Volunteering

Looking at the range of jobs

A deciding factor in what you do will be the amount of time you have available. Maybe you can only spare an hour or two here and there and can never predict when it will be. You may have a regular night each week that you can devote, or it may only be once a year when you feel you can do something.

Below are examples of the voluntary work that could be available to you:

◆ Dropping leaflets for a political party; doing a street collection for a charity; campaigning (from writing letters to going on demonstrations) for an environment group; organising a crèche for local children.

◆ Working at an animal rescue centre or on a city farm; clearing waste from canals or designing a garden for a local community.

◆ Working in a charity shop, or driving a van for an organisation that collects old clothing, furniture and bric-a-brac.

◆ Supporting people in ways such as befriending, counselling, giving telephone support/advice, working for hospital radio.

◆ Learning skilled work on heritage restoration, archae-ological digs or countryside maintenance projects.

◆ Using first aid skills with St John Ambulance or helping to keep people safe as a lifeboat volunteer or mountain rescue worker.

◆ Helping a particular group of people such as those with special needs – for example, the disabled, the homeless, ethnic minorities; this could be one-to-one or group work – anything from being a helper, to going on soup runs, to teaching English as a foreign language.

* As a trustee or committee member you could be using your management/technical/organisational knowledge to help an organisation run properly or to set up a project.

* Doing almost any of the jobs listed under the 'Getting paid work' section earlier in this chapter. Small organisations with very tight resources are often very grateful for volunteers able to provide specialist skills.

WORKING AT HOME OR ABROAD

Working within the voluntary sector in the UK is something that you can do at any time, especially if you are volunteering. But working overseas means you will have to make a commitment of a block of time.

If you decide to find work in the UK (paid or unpaid) you will need to decide where you want to work:

* *Regionally* – paid positions may be difficult to come by, though there will be lots of volunteer opportunities.

* *In London* – some voluntary positions provide food, accommodation and an allowance – and London is where a vast number of the paid positions are.

* *In an urban area* – there are a lot more opportunities than in rural areas.

* *In a rural area* – unless you live in a rural area, opportunities may be limited to weekend work or 'holiday' projects.

Working in the voluntary sector **in the UK** can often provide a useful grounding for working overseas – some organisations insist on it. Firstly, it gives you experience of the voluntary sector culture and, depending on the work you do, it could provide you with experience of dealing with different ethnic cultures.

Working overseas is often seen as more adventurous. It certainly can be interesting to work in a completely different environment and culture. Learning a new language and mixing with different people can be very rewarding. But you need to be realistic about this. For a start, working overseas for only two weeks won't give you the depth or breadth of experience you'd get by working abroad for two years.

Also, if you go overseas with a group of people, it is easy to become complacent and not bother learning the language, or mixing with people from your host country. On the other hand, if you go overseas on your own, even if you learn the language fairly well you could still feel isolated if you can't talk to people about things from your own life.

You may need to sort out permits and visas to work overseas, even as a volunteer. Some organisations will take care of this for you, but many won't. There can be a lot to sort out so you'll need to be well organised and patient.

For more detailed information on working overseas see Chapter 8.

DECIDING HOW LONG TO DO IT FOR

Your commitments/career plans

A family, a serious relationship, a mortgage, loans, pension schemes or any other type of commitment will have an impact on how long you can work in the voluntary sector, whether you are an employee or a volunteer. For example, if you have financial commitments you may have to set some money aside if you want to do a large block of volunteering, or if you want to work on a long-term paid contract overseas. Family members or your partner may feel quite strongly about you working away from home for even a short while.

Your financial commitments may be contributing to your motives to transfer your career to the voluntary sector. You might recognise this as 'wanting to get out of the rat race'. As this means you are thinking about a long-term change, which could see you earning less than you currently do, you will need to work out how you are going to adjust your outgoings so that you can cope. If you say 'I want to get out of the rat race' during an interview, voluntary sector organisations may think you see them as an easy option, so you'll need to convince them that you've thought through the implications of your decision.

If you are at college you might want to do a period of work in the voluntary sector after finishing your studies. You need to think about how long you can spend in the sector without harming your chances of moving into the business world later. For example, if you are an information technology graduate it could be unwise to spend even six months as a volunteer hospital worker in

India; your skills and knowledge could be significantly out of date by the time you return. Even if you are on the paid staff of a voluntary sector organisation in London, setting up its IT systems, you still need to be careful with the time. You may not be dealing with leading edge technology and again, your skills and knowledge could fall significantly behind within a couple of years.

Committing yourself
In most cases the length of time you do voluntary work for is up to you, but some organisations will ask you to make a regular commitment. For example, Relate asks its volunteer counsellors to do at least three hours' counselling each week as well as attend regular training sessions.

All overseas work, paid or not, is temporary. However, contracts can be for a number of years and are sometimes renewable. There is also always the possibility of going from one contract to another.

DECIDING WHEN TO DO IT
- Is your **available time** going to restrict any voluntary work you do? Evenings, weekends, holidays, a particular time of year, a gap year, a secondment, a leave of absence? All these things will affect how flexible you are concerning when you do it.

- How **flexible** are you? If you want to work overseas could you go next month, or, equally possible, are you happy to go in two years' time? Your circumstances could have changed by then, but the application, selection and placement processes for some overseas posts can take many months.

- Is working in the voluntary sector part of a wider **career plan**? If it is, you may need to think about the recruitment processes and needs of your future potential employers to make sure you get your timing right.

- If you are thinking of volunteering, is it something you want to do now or could you do it when you are older, perhaps when you are **retired**?

- Is it something you want to do in your **college holidays**? If it is, it's a good idea to start planning about six months before the holidays start. At the very least you need to investigate the opportunities available to you.

ASSESSING THE BENEFITS

Only you will really know what you are getting out of the experience, whether paid or voluntary, and whether it is enough.

Personal benefits
- job satisfaction
- recognition for contribution
- satisfaction of giving something back
- personal development
- sense of achievement
- new skills and knowledge
- career development
- new friends and social activity
- a sense of belonging
- fun.

Social benefits

◆ *Enhanced quality of life* – whether you are working on a local campaign for better street lighting or a major international project to relieve poverty, the aim will be an enhanced quality of life in some way for someone.

◆ *Community spirit* – by people working together for a 'greater good' the theory is that we'll move towards a more democratic, socially responsible, caring society.

USING THE INTERNET TO MAKE YOUR MARK

If you are unable to spare much time as a volunteer, or do not want to work in the sector, but still want to make a difference, it is possible. The Internet has changed the way many charities operate, including how they raise funds and how they organise campaigns.

For example, some charities have Internet fundraising campaigns where you click on a sponsor's advertisement. Each time you click on the advertisement, the charity receives a small donation. You can also make donations yourself, by filling in online forms.

On many charity websites you can register your concerns about issues, 'sign' petitions and vote on important matters. It helps you to get your point across and the charity benefits by being able to use the information to show relevant bodies the level of concern among the population.

Of course, the Internet is an excellent research tool, particularly for finding volunteer opportunities. One website (www.do-it.org.uk) has a search facility where you can find volunteering opportunities in your area according to the kind of work you are interested in. Another website (www.communtitychannel.org) is specifically for armchair activists.

CASE STUDIES

Mary Neill, St John Ambulance volunteer

'I've been a volunteer now for quite a few years. I enjoy the work side of it – helping people, doing something useful, meeting lots of different people – and getting into football matches free! Seriously though, a lot of the time it's good fun, but it can be upsetting because we can come across some traumatic situations. The thing is, I feel really good when I've helped someone and I can see it in their faces that I've made a difference. I also like the social activities with the other volunteers. My day job's okay, but I don't get the same out of it that I do out of being a volunteer.'

Daniel Cort, archaeology consultant

'I took a leave of absence from my job in London as a museum services archaeologist to work in South America for two years. The museum service promised to keep my job open, but when I got back they made me redundant. It was really strange because before going overseas something like that would have had me fretting about security and money, but I really do think that working overseas made me more relaxed. I found myself enjoying this new challenge and I felt much more confident and flexible. I decided to become self-employed and I now run a small archaeological consultancy.'

Shibero Akatsa-Darby, alcohol abuse counsellor

'I worked as a training consultant in the private sector for ten years. I wanted to be a counsellor, but the leap seemed too large. I decided to take a job as a trainer for a charity. It was a kind of halfway house and it certainly was the right thing to do. I learned a lot about the charity culture and I was exposed to a lot of things going on that I didn't even know about. It gave me exposure to the personal development side of things.

'Making that move gave me a lot of confidence about going into counselling. I really got my act together. I did the Relate training, became a volunteer counsellor and then, as soon as I saw the right job, applied for it and got it. But getting that first charity job is probably the best thing I've ever done because it took me down the path where I'm meant to be going. It kind of concluded my career search.'

CHECKLIST

All the issues in this chapter are interlinked. Your responses to one issue will depend upon your feelings about another. The main points to be aware of are:

◆ Are you clear about why you want to work in the voluntary sector?

◆ Have you thought about your lifestyle and your ambitions?

◆ Are you sure you can adjust to working in the voluntary sector?

◆ Are you looking for a paid position or for voluntary work, and in either case, for how long, where and when?

USEFUL RESOURCES

Further reading

Financial help if you work or are doing voluntary work (leaflet WK4) (Social Security Agency). Leaflet about voluntary work and benefits. Telephone your local Social Security Agency and ask them to send you a copy.

Finding the Right Work for You

APPLYING FOR A JOB

There are a number of ways to apply for paid and voluntary work in the voluntary sector:

- ◆ responding to an advertisement
- ◆ making a speculative application
- ◆ registering with an agency
- ◆ door-knocking.

Speculative applications and door-knocking can work, but because of the attitude towards equal opportunities, they are more useful if you are looking for voluntary work. For speculative applications you will need to write a letter of application and include your CV with it (see Figure 1 for an example of a speculative letter). If you are door-knocking you will need patience and stamina – the better your targeting of organisations the easier your job-hunting will be.

If you see an advertisement for a paid post that interests you, it is likely that you will be asked to complete an application form or to send in your CV. Again, because of equal opportunities, it is important that you do as you are asked. If you are asked to complete an application form, don't send a CV instead. It won't put you at the front of the queue and it could even be ignored. (See Figures 2 to 6 for examples of advertisements and application forms.)

1 Small House
Long Street
Bigtown
BG1 0ZZ

29 June 200X

Ms Spell
Personnel
Big Local Group (BLG)
The High Street
Bigtown
BG1 0AA

Dear Ms Spell

I heard on the radio this week that BLG is raising money to start a vehicle restoration scheme with inner city children. I wonder if there might be any chance to join the staff on the project team and use my vehicle skills?

I am a vehicle mechanic with over 20 years' experience and I have nationally recognised qualifications in vehicle mechanics and electronics. My CV is enclosed.

I worked my way up from apprentice level to managing a large workshop for a national dealer. I have now worked for the AA for several years as a trainer. Although I enjoy this work, I am now looking for a change of direction.

I've been a volunteer helper at a local youth club for many years (I'm still involved). I sometimes run a car maintenance class for the older members and I get a lot of enjoyment seeing them learn new skills. I'd like to do this kind of work on a full-time basis and your project seems an ideal opportunity.

I've read your annual report and I'm very impressed by the work you are doing. I hope you are able to consider my application favourably, and I look forward to hearing from you.

Yours sincerely

Ali Carr

Fig. 1. Sample covering letter for speculative application. *Note* that the writer of this letter has taken the time to do some research – finding the name of the person to contact and getting background information on the organisation.

Fig. 2. Sample advertisement –
Greenpeace.

Fig. 3. Sample advertisement
– Environ

Fig. 4. Sample advertisement
– Winged Fellowship Trust.

For office use only: Ref No.   i.v.:
                            s.u.:

LAMBETH SHAD

VOLUNTEER PERSONAL ASSISTANT – APPLICATION FORM

Please answer the questions below to the best of your ability. In order to assess your application fairly, we need answers to all the questions. We would encourage you to continue any of your answers on another sheet if you feel it will support your application. All of your answers will be treated in the **strictest confidence**.

FULL NAME: (Mr, Ms)...

ADDRESS: ....

....

.... post code..............

TELEPHONE: Day......................... Evening ....

DATE OF BIRTH: .... AGE:..................

NATIONAL INSURANCE NUMBER:......................................

1. WHEN WOULD YOU BE AVAILABLE TO START?.....................

a) How long would you be available for? ....

b) Could you be flexible with these dates?   YES/NO

(If so please specify)..

2. CAN YOU DRIVE?   YES/NO
Is your licence clean and current?   YES/NO

(If not, please say why) ....

....

3. PLEASE GIVE YOUR APPROXIMATE Height........ Weight.........

17/08/07

Fig. 5. Sample volunteer application form – Lambeth SHAD.

ANY HEALTH PROBLEMS? YES/NO

(If yes, please give details), eg: back trouble, allergies etc: ....

....

Please note: Health and safety law is such that you can only work for SHAD if your back is strong and healthy.

4. ARE YOU VEGETARIAN OR VEGAN?   YES/NO

     COULD YOU COOK MEAT FOR SOMEONE ELSE?   YES/NO

5. ARE YOU A SMOKER?   YES/NO

(If YES, roughly how many a day? ....)

     COULD YOU WORK WITH A SMOKER?   YES/NO
     COULD YOU WORK WITH A NON SMOKER?   YES/NO
     COULD YOU LIVE WITH A SMOKER?   YES/NO

6. COULD YOU WORK IN A HOUSEHOLD WITH CATS
     AND DOGS?   YES/NO
7. HAVE YOU EVER BEEN FOUND GUILTY OF A
     CRIMINAL OFFENCE?   YES/NO

If yes, please give details ....

....

(please note this will not necessarily count against you)

8. PLEASE NAME: a) a quality you value in yourself.....................

....

b) a failing you feel you have ....

....

9. IF YOU HAVE DONE ANY VOLUNTARY WORK BEFORE, PLEASE GIVE
DETAILS BELOW (this could be informal, like helping a neighbour with some
shopping, or formal, like helping a voluntary group etc.)

....
....
....

17/08/07

Fig. 5. (continued).

10. PLEASE DESCRIBE HOW YOU SPENT THE LAST YEAR (eg. studies, work, if you have been unemployed, how did you occupy your time?)

....

....

....

....

....

11. PLEASE EXPLAIN WHY THIS PROJECT INTERESTS YOU AND WHAT YOU HOPE TO GAIN BY IT

....

....

....

....

....

....

....

12. PLEASE GIVE DETAILS OF INTERESTS, ACTIVITIES AND ANY FURTHER INFORMATION WHICH YOU MAY FEEL SUPPORT THIS APPLICATION

....

....

....

....

....

....

17/08/97

Fig. 5. (continued).

13. REFEREES PLEASE GIVE THE NAMES AND ADDRESSES OF 2
REFEREES. THEY SHOULD BE PEOPLE YOU RESPECT AND FEEL YOU
KNOW WELL, BUT THEY SHOULD NOT BE MEMBERS OF YOUR FAMILY

Referee 1 (if you are currently on a course, or if you have just finished school
or college this should be a lecturer/teacher who knows you well. If you have
been in a job since leaving your studies, this should be your last employer).

FULL NAME: (Mr, Ms) ....

....

....

....   Post code: ....

TELEPHONE No: ....

THEIR RELATION TO YOU: ....

Referee 2:

FULL NAME: (Mr, Ms) ....

....

....

....   Post code: ....

TELEPHONE No: ....

THEIR RELATION TO YOU: ....

I confirm that all the information on this application is correct to the best of my
knowledge.

SIGNED: ....   DATE.....................

Please return application form, summary sheet and equal opportunities
monitoring form to Lambeth SHAD, Unit 3, The Co-op Centre, 11 Mowll St,
London SW9 6BG.

17/08/97

Fig. 5. (continued).

SHAD

APPLICATION SUMMARY

We sometimes receive more applications than the vacancies we have for Personal Assistants. If we are unable to offer you a post, we may be able to forward your application to other agencies or to disabled individuals, who take on volunteers to work as Personal Assistants. If you are interested in your application being forwarded, please complete this page.

FULL NAME: (Mr, Ms)...

ADDRESS: ....

               .... post code.............

TELEPHONE NO: Day .... Evening ....

DATE OF BIRTH: .... AGE:..................

1. WHEN WOULD YOU BE AVAILABLE TO START?.....................

a) How long would you be available for?...............................

b) Could you be flexible with these dates?   YES/NO

(If so please specify)..

2. CAN YOU DRIVE?   YES/NO
Is your licence clean and current?   YES/NO

(If not, please say why) ....

....

3. PLEASE GIVE YOUR APPROXIMATE Height........   Weight.........

DO YOU CONSIDER YOURSELF FIT AND WELL?   YES/NO
(If no, please give details, eg. back trouble, allergies, etc)
....

4. COULD YOU COOK MEAT FOR SOMEONE ELSE?   YES/NO

5. IF YOU DON'T SMOKE, COULD YOU WORK IN A SMOKING HOUSE?
                                                 YES/NO
IF YOU SMOKE, COULD YOU WORK IN A NON-SMOKING HOUSE?
                                                 YES/NO

17/08/97

Fig. 5. (continued).

APPLICATION FOR EMPLOYMENT
SECTION 1

In line with our Equal Opportunities Policy this section will not be seen by the selection and interviewing panel

POSITION APPLIED FOR

NAME

ADDRESS

POST CODE

TELEPHONE NUMBERS

DAY   EVENING

DO YOU HAVE ANY SPECIAL REQUIREMENTS? PLEASE STATE

Fig. 6. Sample application form for paid position –
Virgina House Settlement.

Please supply the names of two people who are willing to provide a reference in support of your application. One referee should be a current or past employer

NAME

POSITION

ADDRESS

TELEPHONE NUMBER

NAME

POSITION

ADDRESS

TELEPHONE NUMBER

TICK HERE IF YOU WOULD PREFER US NOT TO CONTACT YOUR EMPLOYER BEFORE INTERVIEW? ☐

DECLARATION

I declare that the information submitted in this application form is, to the best of my knowledge, correct. If appointed I understand that any offer of employment will be subject to the receipt of satisfactory references and, if necessary, the satisfactory clearance of the Devon and Cornwall Constabulary under the Rehabilitation of Offenders Act 1974.

SIGNED   DATE

OFFICE USE ONLY			
SELECTED FOR INTERVIEW?	Y / N	INTERVIEW DATE AND TIME	
REFS. REQUESTED		REFS. RECEIVED 1	2
OFFER Y / N SENT		ACCEPT RECEIVED	
COMMENCE DATE		START SALARY	
MANAGER INFORMED		BSU INFORMED	

Fig. 6. (continued).

APPLICATION FOR EMPLOYMENT
SECTION 2

EDUCATION AND TRAINING

Please give details here of any qualifications you have obtained or training undertaken which you believe to be relevant to the fulfilment of the post applied for

DATES FROM/TO	ESTABLISHMENT ATTENDED	QUALIFICATION OR TRAINING	GRADES

PRESENT EMPLOYMENT (IF ANY)

EMPLOYER'S NAME

ADDRESS

TITLE OF POST HELD

DATES EMPLOYED

FULL OR PART-TIME?

Office Use Only   Candidate Number

Fig. 6. (continued).

PLEASE GIVE BRIEF DETAILS HERE OF CURRENT DUTIES

What period of notice are you required to give your employer?

Please give details here of any previous paid employment and experience
(continue on separate sheet if necessary)

DATES	EMPLOYER	TITLE & MAIN DUTIES OF POST

Please give details here of any relevant voluntary service or unpaid work which you have undertaken

DATES	EMPLOYER / AGENCY	WORK UNDERTAKEN

Office Use Only   Candidate Number

Fig. 6. (continued).

PLEASE REFER TO BOTH THE JOB DESCRIPTION AND PERSON SPECIFICATION AND DESCRIBE WHAT SKILLS AND EXPERIENCE YOU HAVE TO SATISFY THE REQUIREMENTS OF THE POST APPLIED FOR
(CONTINUE ON A SEPARATE SHEET IF NECESSARY)

Office Use Only   Candidate Number

Fig. 6. (continued).

BY REFERRING AGAIN TO THE JOB DESCRIPTION AND THE PERSON SPECIFICATION
EXPLAIN HOW YOU WOULD APPROACH THE WORK AND STATE WHAT IDEAS YOU HAVE
FOR DEVELOPING THE POST APPLIED FOR
(CONTINUE ON A SEPARATE SHEET IF NECESSARY)

REHABILITATION OF OFFENDERS ACT 1974

This post will entail significant access to children and vulnerable persons. Certain provisions
of the Rehabilitation of Offenders Act do not apply to this post and thus any successful
candidate will be required to disclose any criminal convictions they may have including those
normally deemed to be 'spent' under the 1974 Act. Any offer of appointment made will be
subject to satisfactory clearance being obtained from the Devon and Cornwall Constabulary.
It should be noted that having a criminal record does not in itself disbar any candidate from
appointment. Candidates are ensured that all disclosures will be dealt with in the strictest
confidence.

PLEASE ENSURE THAT YOU HAVE COMPLETED EVERY PART OF THIS APPLICATION FORM IN ACCORDANCE WITH THE
NOTES *HOW TO COMPLETE THE APPLICATION FORM.*
WHEN COMPLETE RETURN BOTH SECTIONS TO

VIRGINIA HOUSE SETTLEMENT, 40 LOOE STREET. BRETONSIDE. PLYMOUTH PL4 0EB

Office Use Only   Candidate Number

Fig. 6. (continued).

But whatever way you make an approach, it is important that you are clear about your own skills, experience and suitability for the work.

FITTING IN YOUR LIFESTYLE AND ASPIRATIONS

If you are considering paid work in the voluntary sector, thinking about your life as it is now and as you want it to be in the future is an important part of your career planning. It will be worth doing the following exercises to focus your mind on what you want to get out of your experience. Even if you are only considering volunteering you may still find these exercises useful in helping to decide what kind of volunteering you want to do.

Thinking about your life now

Take some time to do this exercise. It's worth spending a couple of hours doing it initially and it may be worth coming back to it, as you read through the rest of this book.

Exercise

Write yourself some notes in response to these questions:

1. What do you like/dislike about your current work?

2. How much are you paid and is it enough? If not, how much could you realistically aim for?

3. Write a paragraph describing your typical working day. Note down your start and finish times; the routine tasks; the challenging tasks; who you meet; the interactions you have with colleagues. Write down how you feel about what you do, when you do it, why you do it.

4. How much free time do you have outside work and what do you do with your free time? Make a list and

note down the main features of each thing – is it competitive, creative, co-operative, social, isolated, active, passive, a chore?

5. Why do you do these things – what is it that you like about them?

6. Finally, make a list of the things that have happened to you or that you have done that you feel have shaped your life.

Thinking about your future

It may be hard to visualise yourself in five or ten years time but try to picture yourself that far ahead for this exercise. Imagine that time is not a constraint and, in terms of work and lifestyle, you can do whatever you want. Describe your dream job and include the following:

◆ What the work would be and how much responsibility you would have.

◆ Who you would be working for.

◆ How many days a week you would work.

◆ How much you would be paid.

◆ Where (country and town) you would be living and what kind of house and transport you would have.

◆ What kind of people would be around you.

◆ How you would spend your free time.

Imagine you are writing a list in a few years time of things you have done. What would you like them to be?

Being realistic

Now take these exercises and look at what they say about you. Are you materialistic, competitive, a leader, a loner, a socialiser? Do you respond to deadlines or hate them? And so on. The idea is to have a starting point for understanding what motivates you. Be honest with yourself. If money is important to you, there is nothing wrong with that, but depending on how important it is, it might mean that paid work in the voluntary sector is not for you. You still might be able to make a great contribution as a volunteer and have some wonderful experiences along the way. If you are honest with yourself, these exercises should help you decide, not just whether you want paid or voluntary work, but what kind of work you want it to be.

KNOWING WHAT YOU HAVE TO OFFER

If you spend some time thinking about your skills, experience, personality and background, the information that you come up with will be useful when you apply for jobs and when you go to interviews.

If you are having a conversation with a friend you might say, for example, 'I'm good at hockey'. After a little more conversation you might agree with your friend that you're good at hockey because you are competitive and disciplined and you are able to motivate your team-mates when the going gets tough. For applications and interviews it's these last bits of information that are important and that you need ready to hand.

The exercises in this section will help you to identify in a clear and well-ordered way what you have to offer.

Listing your experience

Exercise

1. Take a pen and a few blank sheets of A4 paper and write down as many positive things as you can from your life experience. Write down things from your whole experience – personal, social, work, travel, sports and so on. Write them down as they come to you and write anywhere on the page. Doing it this way will stop you writing a list of points one under the other and this is important because it will allow your mind to wander and make associations. This is more creative than list-making and you'll probably find you get more information this way.

2. Now take two coloured pens and put different coloured rings around things depending on whether they are work or non-work experiences.

3. Take a big sheet of blank paper (A3 or bigger) and draw three columns on it. At the top of the first column put 'EXPERIENCE'. Underneath this take all the things you have ringed as work and put them into a chronological order. Then continue underneath with the non-work experience.

You should now have a good list of your experience and achievements.

Listing your skills

Exercise

1. Take another sheet of A4 paper and list all the skills you can think of that you have and use in all the

different areas of your life. Again write them down randomly.

2. Go back to your large sheet of paper and at the top of the second column write 'SKILLS'. Underneath this write down all the skills that you came up with, against the experiences where they have been used.

You should now be getting a picture of where your skills and experience match up and prove each other.

Listing your personal qualities
Exercise

1. Again on a blank sheet of A4 write down randomly, in any order on the page, all the positive personal qualities that you have. Don't be modest.

2. Then, on your large sheet of paper write 'PERSONAL QUALITIES' at the top of the third column and list underneath, in line with the experiences, all your qualities.

What you now have is a template for future job applications and interviews (see Figure 7). If you have any gaps, see if they can be filled. For example, if an experience doesn't have any skills or personal qualities lined up with it, spend some time thinking about what skills and qualities that experience demonstrates that you have, and fill in those gaps.

Now, when you are applying for jobs, instead of each time thinking how you match up to a job description or how you can answer a particular question, you will have something to refer to. You can add to it as you gather new experiences and achievements.

EXPERIENCE	SKILLS	QUALITIES
Market stall job – selling fabric	Selling/Display Money/Customer service	Honest/Punctual Hard-working (cold winters)/People-person
Passed driving test first time	Driving/ Coordination Concentration	Determined
Passed 9 GCSEs	Study skills/Time-management	Intelligent/Good learner
Café job – cooking, waiting on tables, cashing up	Teamwork/Cooking Customer service Basic bookkeeping Cleaning	Hard-working Practical/Friendly Willing to learn Hands-on Determined (saving money to go to USA)
USA – travel/ stayed with pen-friend	Budgeting/Map reading Initiative/Planning Organising	Adventurous Outgoing/Flexible Resourceful/Fun
Night shift shop work – motorway services	Selling/supervising Display/Cash handling Interpersonal (abusive customers) Customer Service	Hard working/ Flexible/Calm/ People-person
Passed typing exam	Typing/letter writing	Focused/ Determined Willing to learn

Fig. 7. Sample experience, skills and qualities template.

Another value of this exercise is that often, on application forms and in interviews, you will be asked for evidence of the qualities and skills that you say you have. This exercise gives you that evidence in the first column.

WRITING YOUR CV
Another good thing about the last set of exercises is that you will be able to use them for writing up your CV.

There are a number of theories about how you should present your CV, but whichever approach you take, keep it:

1. clear
2. brief
3. relevant.

Keeping it clear
+ don't use jargon
+ use short sentences
+ type or word process your CV using black ink
+ use white paper
+ use a clear, easy-to-read font
+ don't use lots of bold, italics or underlining.

Keeping it brief
Keep your CV short and no more than two sides of A4 at most. Remember that the person reading it at the other end may have hundreds of applications and a tight deadline – a long CV could lose the reader by page three.

Keeping it relevant
Making your CV relevant to the position you are applying for is very important. This is why a template like the one

discussed earlier is useful. You won't want to put everything from it on your CV, so you can pick and choose according to the skills required in the job you are applying for.

If you are making a speculative application you won't be able to tailor your CV to any particular job, so it's important to do some general research about the organisation to know what kind of things are important to it. It's also important to be clear about what kind of work you want.

Presenting your CV

The way you present your CV is your first opportunity to make a good impression. A well-presented CV tells the reader that the applicant is smart, self-disciplined and organised, that you don't waffle and that you might be the right person for the job.

You need to include:

◆ your name and address
◆ your work history
◆ your education
◆ any special achievements or skills that are relevant.

You can put referees on your CV, but if you need to run on to three pages just to put them on, it probably isn't worth including them. Also you don't need to put 'CV' or 'Curriculum Vitae' at the top of your CV – it takes up space and it's obvious what it is anyway. (See Figure 8 for an example of a CV layout.)

Sue Frances

Sue Frances, 51 Tall Street, London N1 2A Tel: (020) 8123 5678

WORK EXPERIENCE

FACILITATING   Recruited and led a committee of professionals to manage a major new marketing initiative. Coordinated cross-unit working groups within the company on a range of projects, such as policy formulation for use of images. Trained staff and volunteers in dealing with the public, corporate image etc. Developed links between British and Peruvian schools. Designed and organised events to raise profile and involve people.

COMMUNICATING   Planned and implemented media campaigns, wrote press releases, gave radio interviews. Made presentations and gave talks to groups. Wrote and produced promotional materials – direct mail, annual reports, newsletters. Conducted interviews with people at all levels, from government officials to Peruvian villagers. Researched and installed systems to enable more effective marketing and better servicing of customers.

MANAGING   Designed and developed a supporters association to increase fundraising and publicity potential from individuals. Initiated and carried out appeals to individuals, groups, and trusts, achieving fundraising targets. Monitored and evaluated all fundraising and PR projects. Designed and coordinated direct mail recruitment campaigns.

WORK HISTORY

1994 – present   Charity for Peru, London
Information Officer
Public Relations, Fundraising, Marketing

1987 – 1994   Volunteers Abroad, London
Fundraising and Public Relations Assistant

1985 – 1987   Secretary

1984 – 1985   Clerk Typist

EDUCATION/TRAINING

1993   Open University
Winning Resources and Support (Management Certificate Course)
The Effective Manager (Management Certificate Course)

1983 – 1984   BTEC Diploma in Business Studies, RSA Typing II, RSA Shorthand 80wpm

Fig. 8. Sample CV.

FILLING OUT THE APPLICATION FORM

There are a number of points to consider:

- Before filling in the application form properly, either take a copy of it and fill that in, or fill in the original in pencil. This way you can make mistakes on a practice run.

- Use black ink or type (it photocopies more clearly) unless asked to do something different.

- Write in block capitals where possible unless asked to use your own handwriting.

- Keep within the space given unless the form indicates you can use extra sheets – but, as with CVs, it's a good idea to keep things brief.

- Don't use jargon.

- Don't write 'see CV' unless you are asked or given permission to include one with your application form.

- Read all the information sent with the application form and make your response to the questions relevant.

- Keep a photocopy of your completed application form for your reference.

REGISTERING WITH AN AGENCY

There are several specialist agencies that help to place people either as volunteers or as paid workers.

Volunteers

In almost every town in the country you will find some

organisation that knows what is going on in your area in terms of voluntary work. It could be a volunteer bureau, a citizens' advice bureau, your local information office or your local library. They will have noticeboards and stocks of leaflets with information about volunteer groups and projects.

Volunteer bureaux are run slightly differently from town to town. Some operate registers or lists of people who want to find volunteer positions. To get on the register all you have to do is call in at your local bureau, fill in a form and have a short discussion with one of the staff. This will help them to see what your skills and interests are so they can match you up with the right kind of organisation. Of course, the choice is yours, because you can say what kind of organisation you are interested in and you don't have to accept the first thing that's offered.

The charity REACH operates as a linking service between late career/early retirement professionals looking for voluntary work and voluntary organisations that may need their skills. The 'linked' individuals work on an expenses-only basis. If you want to do voluntary work overseas there are several agencies you could contact and some useful addresses are listed in Chapter 8.

If you want to be a trustee you could register with Charity Appointments (see below).

For more information on finding voluntary work see Chapter 5.

Paid workers

There are several agencies specialising in charity recruitment, though you could always contact one of the many high street recruitment consultancies to see what services they offer. The agencies specialising in charity recruitment are:

- CF Appointments
- Charity Connections
- Charity People
- Charity Recruitment.

CF Appointments (also known as Charity and Fundraising Appointments) is a charity operating a recruitment consultancy for executive and trustee appointments in the voluntary sector. If you are in this category, looking for a voluntary sector position, you should send your CV with a covering letter, outlining the kind of work desired and your salary expectations.

Charity Connections recruits temporary and permanent positions for the voluntary sector. It specialises in office staff from clerical through to senior management levels.

Charity People recruits for the voluntary sector in the following areas: administration, senior administration, chief executive, communications, finance, fundraising, IT, management and marketing.

Charity Recruitment has a register of experienced people who are actively seeking work in the voluntary sector. It also runs a search and selection service for voluntary sector organisations.

Voluntary sector organisations operating registers of potential overseas workers can be found in Chapter 8.

HANDLING THE INTERVIEW

It may seem trivial, but one of the most troubling things when going to an interview at a voluntary sector organisation can be deciding what to wear. To an extent it depends on the organisation and the job you are going for – firstly whether it's voluntary or paid. If you are going for a job as a finance director in a major charity it would be unwise to wear sandals and jeans. But if you wanted a volunteer place on an archaeological dig a suit would be inappropriate (and uncomfortable). Smart and casual is acceptable for most interviews, though if you are at all unsure, simply phone up and ask what's expected.

There are three keys to handling an interview well:

1. preparation
2. personal comfort
3. listening skills.

Being prepared

If you are invited to an interview you need to know:

- what it is for
- when it is
- where it is
- how it will be done
- what they will be looking for.

Some organisations are very good at keeping people informed and you will have all this information in the invitation to the interview, or even before. For example, some organisations, when they send you an information pack, will include a person specification indicating at what stages they will be looking for different things (see Chapter 6 for more about this).

However, if you are not sure, telephone the organisation and ask questions such as:

♦ Which post am I being considered for? (If you have applied for more than one.)

♦ How many interviews will I have?

♦ How many interviewers will there be in each interview?

♦ How long will each interview last?

♦ What will each interview cover? (Don't expect a detailed answer, but it's useful to know which interview is covering personal issues and which one is focusing on your skills.)

♦ Will there be any activities/tasks and what sort?

♦ Do I need to bring anything with me (for example, certificates or portfolio)?

Having this kind of information will mean that you are not taken by surprise if you are faced with a panel of five interviewers when you were expecting only one. It will also mean you can plan your return journey in advance if you know how long you can expect to be kept for – and that's one less thing to worry about on the day.

Also, once you have the information you can do some rehearsing:

- If possible, travel to the interview location before the interview date to be sure of where you are going and to see how long it will take you to get there.

- Decide what clothes you will wear and make sure they are in good condition for the day.

- Look through the job description, the person specification and other information and write out a list of questions that you would ask if you were the interviewer.

- Write out a list of questions that you would like to ask the interviewers.

Figure 9 gives a sample of some questions you might be asked during an interview for almost any position in the voluntary sector.

Being comfortable

Make sure you arrive for the interview or selection day a good 15 minutes in advance of the start time, so that you feel relaxed and comfortable. Take something with you to read in the gaps between interviews and exercises – something light or humorous will keep you relaxed and make you feel more positive. Also take a snack with you in case there are no biscuits available when you arrive; it's amazing how tiring interviews are, so it's useful to keep your energy levels up if you can snack between. But don't eat chocolate bars – small bits of chocolate melting on your clothes does not create the right image!

SAMPLE INTERVIEW QUESTIONS

Tell me about your education.

Tell me about your work/voluntary work at . . . .

Having seen the job description what do you think are the most important skills needed to do the job?

Why do you want to do this kind of work?

How did you come to be interested in the issues we deal with?

What drives you?

What do you think are the main differences between working in the voluntary sector and working in the commercial sector?

Give me an example of a situation that has put you under stress. What did you do?

What do you most enjoy in your work?

What do you most dislike in your work?

What experience of equal opportunities do you have?

Tell me about a difficulty that you encountered working with a colleague/client.

> These are very general questions that could be asked for any job in any voluntary sector organisation. They're not as tame as they look – expect interviewers to probe further once you've given an answer. There will always be specific questions relating to the position you are applying for. Don't be surprised if you are asked to complete tests or take part in group activities.

Fig. 9. Sample interview questions.

If you need to go to the toilet make sure you go in plenty of time before you are called in to the interview. If you have just poured yourself a drink ask if it's all right to take it with you into the interview. But never eat, smoke or chew gum in an interview – don't even ask.

Listening skills

Listening is an important part of communication skills, if not the most vital one. During an interview or assessment exercise you will need to use your listening skills to their utmost:

◆ Listen with full attention to what is being said.

◆ If you do not understand something or think you may have misheard, ask for clarification.

◆ Answer the question that you are asked.

◆ Be aware of any subtle body language signals the interviewers may give to show they have heard enough – draw your point to a rapid conclusion and wait for the next question.

During the day

Being interviewed
Just because you have applied to a voluntary sector organisation, don't expect an easy ride as far as interviews and other selection procedures are concerned.

◆ Whatever documents you take in with you, make sure they are organised and relevant.

◆ Have a copy of your application form to hand and don't be afraid to look at it or refer to it.

- Clarify at the start whether there will be time at the end for you to ask questions or if you can ask questions as you go along (the first is more usual).

- Have a large notepad to hand and several pens available. Don't be afraid to take notes during the interview; there may be something you want to come back to when you get your chance to ask questions. This notepad should be where your prepared questions are written down.

- Stay relaxed, talk clearly, be brief, don't ramble, and keep good eye contact with your interviewers – smile, it may be difficult but it helps.

- If the interviewer asks for evidence of something you say, it is important that you come up with something (this is where the exercises under 'Knowing what you have to offer' come in useful).

Doing assessment exercises

Assessment exercises can take different forms, from psychometric tests to problem-solving in groups. If you have to do an assessment exercise it's important not to try to second-guess what the assessors are looking for. For example, you may be going for a management position and have to do a group exercise or discussion. If your previous experience has been in a tough commercial environment it would be easy to assume that the assessors are looking for the kinds of qualities that helped you survive there. But remember, voluntary sector culture is different. The only real answer is to be yourself and not to act out a role.

Also, in some assessment exercises it may seem to you as though you have been over the same ground in other exercises or interviews. There will be good reasons for this and the assessors/interviewers will be looking for different things each time.

Following the interview day

Before you leave an interview, ask when you can expect to hear the results. If you haven't heard anything by the given date make a phone call to find out what's happened.

If you haven't been successful, make sure that you ask for some feedback on your performance. Then you'll have something to work on and improve for the next time.

CASE STUDIES

Chris Black, student

'I left school and did an HND in computing and then went straight to work for an IT company. I didn't really think about it, it just seemed the obvious thing to do. The problem was I stopped enjoying it.

'So I started thinking about what I wanted in life. I did some career planning and took a good look at what I'm really interested in.

'I've done a lot of two-week stints of volunteering on conservation projects over the past six years and really enjoyed it. Last year I got involved in some of the public relations work for the organisation. Nothing much, but enough to give me an insight – and I got a real buzz when I wrote a press release and the story appeared in the local paper.

'There are lots of other things as well, but in a way it was that that made me realise how much conservation issues matter to me and how much I enjoy talking to people about them. I knew I didn't have the technical knowledge to get one of the more scientific jobs, but I realised I was good at getting messages across. I looked into public relations courses and now I'm back at college doing a PR qualification. My aim is to get a PR or information job with a conservation or wildlife group.'

Jane Biggs, recruitment officer, international charity

'I think what I find amazing is the number of people who seem to put no thought into their application. Maybe they expect that because we're a charity it's OK to send the form in a bit crumpled, to write illegibly, or to ignore instructions.

'For example, it says quite clearly on our application form "do not send a CV", but people still do and they just write in the boxes on the application form "see CV". They get rejected.

'The most amazing one, though, was the doctor who wrote "GP" under the job title column and "self-evident" under the description of duties column. My speciality is recruiting people so it's not my job to make assumptions and that means that nothing that anyone does is self-evident.

'Generally, by the time we get people to the assessment centre stage, we have a pretty good bunch of candidates. But there's sometimes one who interrupts to answer a question before we've finished asking it; or they try to take control of a group exercise – generally they come across as arrogant and insensitive.

'I think the one piece of advice I'd give to anyone applying to work in the voluntary sector is to try to think about the person at the other end, the person who's going to look at your application form or interview you. You're going to have to use all your communication skills to their best and that means following instructions, listening skills, empathy, clarity – in other words, a lot of hard work.'

CHECKLIST

◆ Where do you want to be in five or ten years time?

◆ What motivates you?

◆ What skills do you have and can you back them up through experiences?

◆ Is your CV brief, clear and relevant?

◆ What should you remember when filling in an application form?

◆ How can you prepare for an interview?

USEFUL RESOURCES

Useful addresses

CF Appointments Ltd, Lloyds Court, 1 Goodman's Yard, London E1 8AT. Tel: (020) 7953 1191. www.cfappoointments.com
Email: enquiries@cfappointments.com

Charity Connections Recruitment Services, 15 Theed Street, Waterloo, London SE1 8ST. Tel: (020) 7202 9000. www.charityconnections.co.uk
Email: info@charityconnections.co.uk

Charity People, 38 Bedford Place, Bloomsbury, London WC1B 5JH. Tel: (020) 7299 8700.
www.charitypeople.co.uk

Charity Recruitment, 40 Rosebery Avenue, London EC1R 4RN. Tel: (020) 7833 0770.
www.charityrecruitment.co.uk
E-mail: enquiries@charityrecruit.co.uk

REACH, 89 Albert Embankment, London SE1 7TP. Tel: (020) 7582 6543. www.volwork.org.uk
E-mail: mail@reach-online.org.uk

Further reading

How to Write a Winning CV: A New Way to Succeed, Alan Jones (Random House Business Books, 2001).

Teach Yourself Winning at Job Interviews, Igor Popovich (Hodder-Arnold, 2003).

Successful Interviews Every Time, Dr Rob Yeung (How To Books, 2004).

Write a Winning CV: Essential CV Writing Skills that Will Get You the Job You Want, Julie-Ann Amos (How To Books, 2003).

The Perfect Cover Letter, Richard H Beatty (John Wiley & Sons Inc, 2003).

What Colour is Your Parachute? A Practical Manual for Job Hunters and Career Changers, Richard Bolles (Ten Speed Press, 1999).

(4)

Looking at Opportunities for Young People

ACQUIRING NEW SKILLS, CONFIDENCE, RESPONSIBILITY

As a young person in your teens or early to mid-20s, you may be keen to get into work and start earning money – but you are probably all too aware of the catch-22 of 'no experience – no job – no job – no experience'. Also, you may feel it's important to make your mark on society and play an active role in improving the world around you. The voluntary sector can provide you with valuable experience that will:

♦ add something valuable to your CV
♦ develop new skills
♦ give you responsibility
♦ develop your resourcefulness
♦ give you independence
♦ boost your confidence
♦ widen your circle of friends
♦ provide adventure
♦ give you a chance to make a contribution.

If you are still at college, voluntary work can provide you with experience that shows to potential employers that you have the right attitude. The good thing about voluntary work is that you can often choose to do something that's very relevant to what you want to do later on. So, for example, if you want to go into nursing or health service management then voluntary work with children, the elderly or the disabled, or volunteering with an organisation like St John Ambulance, would show commitment to a caring profession and relevant experience.

If you are out of work or looking for your first paid job, the voluntary sector can be a good place to start, but it's important not to think it's an easy option. Many voluntary sector organisations need people with real skills, so again, earlier voluntary work will be useful. Some people decide to work in the voluntary sector for a few years before moving into the private sector – they feel it is a chance to do something worthwhile and it gives them a whole range of skills that will be useful later on.

Getting new skills
Depending on the type of organisation you work for and the kind of work you do, there are lots of possibilities for developing new skills. A lot of voluntary sector organisations take training (of volunteers and paid workers) very seriously.

♦ *Office skills* – word processing, spreadsheets, filing, reception duties, using office equipment, understanding office administration, bookkeeping, report writing, telephone skills and so on.

♦ *Practical skills* – cooking, car maintenance, hedge laying, farming, surveying, nursing, teaching, film-making, decorating, sailing, building and many more.

◆ *People skills* – dealing with people from all walks of life, listening, supporting, motivating, encouraging, sorting out conflicts, facilitating, negotiating.

◆ *Initiative* – for some voluntary work, such as Raleigh International, you will have to raise sponsorship money before you can take part. The ability to achieve this shows initiative and persistence as well as skills associated with fundraising (communication, publicity, organising, prioritising, setting and meeting targets and so on).

Increasing confidence

Again it depends on the kind of organisation you are working for, but working in the voluntary sector can increase your confidence, not only because of the challenges you face, but because the voluntary sector culture tends to be more supportive of people as people rather than just as workers.

◆ Training in things like assertiveness and work skills will help you gain confidence.

◆ Dealing with people from all kinds of backgrounds will expose you to all kinds of ideas and situations.

◆ Working with limited resources is challenging. For example, working with others to meet what might seem like impossible fundraising targets, and meeting that challenge, will boost your skills and confidence.

◆ Living away from home on residential volunteering schemes, whether in the UK or overseas, will boost your independence and your self-esteem.

Getting responsibility

If you want extra responsibility you have to be able to show your commitment and ability to do it, but most organisations are quite small so the opportunities to take this on and to get involved in things like small projects can occur quite frequently.

◆ 'Managing' – you could be working in a charity shop pricing articles, setting up window displays and dealing with customers; you might end up supervising other volunteers and training new ones.

◆ Leading a group – you could be asked to work on developing a newsletter or organising an exhibition, publicity event or even a campaign, and to get other people involved.

◆ You might get training in conservation and leadership skills and then use those skills with different groups of people, from local school children to visiting dignitaries.

◆ You could get involved with a local interest group – perhaps a campaign for street lighting or a political party – and be involved in gathering evidence and putting a case forward and presenting arguments.

On the other hand, if you want to do something where you just turn up and do some work for a good cause, without taking on responsibility, there are plenty of these opportunities too.

WORKING IN YOUR GAP YEAR OR DURING VACATIONS

A good time to do a concentrated burst of work (voluntary or paid) is during your vacations or your 'gap' year.

Paid vacation work in the voluntary sector can be difficult to get, but if you are fairly targeted in your approach, do your research well and have useful skills it can be done. Also, you could register with a high street temporary recruitment agency and let them know this is the kind of work you are interested in – but you should have typing and word processing skills to stand a real chance.

Voluntary vacation work is much easier to get and there are lots of organisations that take people to work on projects or schemes for days, weeks or months at a time, both in the UK and overseas. It can be a good opportunity to meet people from other parts of the country (or world even) and to really get away from it all while still doing something worthwhile and that you can put on your CV.

If the work is residential you might have to make a financial contribution to get a place, though some organisations will pay you a living allowance while you are working.

The gap year is traditionally taken between leaving school and going to university. But don't feel this is what you have to do. There are lots of ways of doing it and here are some ideas:

◆ Leave school, work for a couple of years, take a year out to volunteer overseas and then return to work or go to college.

- Go straight to college and take a gap year after getting your qualification.

- Get your qualifications, work for a few years and then take a gap year.

- Get your qualifications through a modular course that you can 'stop-start'. This may mean doing your studies part-time or by distance-learning (as with the Open University) while working, but the advantage will be that you can earn money while you study and be very flexible about when you do any volunteering.

The jobs market is getting more and more flexible, so you can do things like this when it's right for you, rather than when it's traditional.

Working in the UK
- It will be easier to get paid work in the voluntary sector.

- If you have to move away from home, whether volunteering or doing a paid job, you will still have your support networks fairly close.

- You can 'sample' the experience by volunteering for an organisation at weekends.

Working overseas
- It will be virtually impossible to get paid work without substantial work experience.

- You have little chance of getting a taste of the experience before you commit yourself to it.

- Doing voluntary work overseas could look better on your CV than backpacking around the world with no particular aim.

♦ You should think about whether you are going to organise the work before you depart from the UK or
when you arrive in a particular country. In many ways
it will be easier and safer to do it from the UK, though
it may not seem as adventurous. Either way you will
have to make sure you have all the right paperwork (visas, work permits and so on) before you go.

See Chapter 8 if you want to explore this option further.

DOING PAID WORK IN THE VOLUNTARY SECTOR – IS IT A REAL JOB?

You may decide that you want a career, or at least your
first paid job, in the voluntary sector. You might face
challenges from friends and family who believe that it's
not a 'real' job. This kind of attitude tends to follow from
a lack of understanding of the sector and how it works.

Of course, if you do want to work in the sector it's
important to be clear about your own motives, what you
can offer and what you expect to get out of it (see
Chapters 2 and 3). If you do work in the sector,
occasionally when you tell people they will say things
like 'do you get paid for that?' as if you had another 'real'
job.

So here are some useful things to know if you, your
friends or family are concerned that working in the
voluntary sector isn't part of the real world:

♦ Salaries in the voluntary sector range from below
£10,000 to over £100,000.

- Voluntary sector organisations have contracts of employment, terms and conditions, disciplinary and grievance procedures, appraisals, trade union representation and many other things you would expect to find in a place of work.

- People working in the voluntary sector, like those in other sectors, make decisions about budgets, targets, policies and so on.

- People in voluntary sector organisations make decisions that affect the lives of others – sometimes they are life and death decisions.

- Some people in the voluntary sector have the ear of politicians, journalists, dignitaries, and industrialists. . . . In other words they can have a lot of influence.

UNDERSTANDING GOVERNMENT SCHEMES

All governments are concerned to keep unemployment low and to get people back into work. A number of schemes have been devised over the years to do this and the most successful has been the New Deal.

The New Deal began as something for the under-25 age group. However, it is now open to unemployed people of all ages, and the scheme is divided up to meet specific needs. For example, there is a scheme to help lone parents get back to work.

Under the New Deal scheme you are placed with an employer for six months and during that time you receive training and a wage or an allowance. Many New Deal schemes are run by voluntary sector organisations, so if you want to work in this sector and are currently unemployed it may be worth asking your employment adviser about this.

Another scheme is very new. It was announced in the government's 2005 Budget and is called National Community Service. It will pay a living allowance for young people wanting to take a year out to do community-oriented volunteer work, and will also provide support for people wanting to try shorter term volunteering. At the time of writing there are no details about how this scheme will be run so it may be worth checking on the Home Office website at: www.homeoffice.gov.uk.

The advantages of working in the voluntary sector through government schemes tend to be:

◆ you get paid
◆ you learn new skills
◆ you get work experience to put on your CV
◆ you get training and possibly qualifications
◆ you get references
◆ to gain a knowledge of issues and voluntary sector culture
◆ it could be a stepping stone to your next job
◆ you could get taken on permanently.

HEARING WHAT PRIVATE AND PUBLIC SECTOR EMPLOYERS THINK

The majority of employers don't look specifically for voluntary experience or experience of paid work in the voluntary sector. However, when applicants put it on their forms most employers seem keen to discuss it at interview. A small survey of private and public sector employers (ranging from the NHS to fast food chains) was carried out for this book. Below are the questions that were asked and a sample of the responses.

Looking for new staff – do employers look for evidence of involvement in voluntary activities?

◆ 'Yes, it demonstrates motivation to work, ability to associate with people from different backgrounds, and the experiences contribute to the individual's personal development.'

◆ 'I do look for this. I look for evidence that the candidate has personally developed in some way; for example, listening skills through the Samaritans, teamwork if staffing an Oxfam shop, etc.'

◆ 'We don't specifically look for involvement in voluntary activities, but if people have been involved we're interested in talking about it.'

◆ 'Voluntary work may be useful as experience of some work or as demonstrating commitment.'

Giving advice to someone considering voluntary activity – what do employers say?

◆ 'Work in an area which interests you on a regular and consistent basis; seek to hold positions of responsibility; demonstrate your dependability, use of initiative, confidentiality, etc.'

◆ 'Consider what you could learn from the experience. Will it help you develop in areas where you might otherwise not have any experience?'

◆ 'Choose a function or an organisation which has some relevance to your career plans.'

Thinking about paid workers in the voluntary sector – what do employers say?

◆ 'There's no reason to suppose that voluntary sector work is less stressful or team-oriented than other types of work.'

◆ 'Skills acquired in the voluntary sector are often transferable to other sectors. The internal politics in voluntary organisations can provide useful insights into public sector organisations.'

◆ 'I would expect any voluntary organisation would be a very well-organised and cost-effective business, due to reliance on donations, etc. for the business to function.'

Developing useful skills and attributes in the voluntary sector – what do employers think?

◆ 'It develops similar skills to commercial employment.'

◆ 'Voluntary sector work can provide opportunities to take responsibility, to work in or lead teams and to make a real impact.'

◆ 'Depending upon the role it can help leadership, planning and organisation, initiative and financial awareness.'

◆ 'Teamwork, communication skills, creativity, awareness of limited resources, valuing staff.'

LOOKING AT WHAT YOU CAN DO

Paid work

As a young person, with perhaps not much work experience, it can be difficult to find a job that matches your aspirations anywhere, not just in the voluntary sector. Having said that, the voluntary sector is so big and diverse that there are plenty of opportunities to get that all-important 'foot in the door' position from where you can move on.

If you want to work for one of the very big organisations that are household names, it is likely that you will have to move to London or the south of England because this is where most of them are based. However, some of them do have offices in the regions. Remember that competition for posts with organisations like Action Aid, NSPCC or Friends of the Earth is fierce and they are able to pick and choose from the best applicants.

When you are applying for jobs you need to be realistic about what you can and can't do, and if your application is rejected it is always worth phoning up to see if you can get some feedback. It may be better to apply for a more mundane position, in a department you are interested in, to get a foot in the door. Something that will give your application an edge is having relevant voluntary work experience.

Voluntary work

The number of things you can do as a volunteer is countless whatever age you are. The good thing about being young is that there are schemes specially set up to encourage you to volunteer, and many voluntary organisations particularly welcome young volunteers.

- *BUNAC (British Universities North America Club)* – provides opportunities for young people to work and travel throughout the world.

- *CSV (Community Service Volunteers)* – full-time residential volunteering. CSV trains unemployed people for careers in community care, horticulture, building, tourism and enterprise.

- *European Voluntary Service* – open to people between the ages of 18 and 25 living in the European Union. Provides opportunities to spend between six and twelve months in another EU country working on a social, environmental or cultural project.

- *Gap Activity Projects (GAP)* – sends school-leavers on volunteer projects in over 30 countries, teaching English, doing conservation/outdoor work and social/caring work.

- *IVS (International Voluntary Service)* – co-ordinates workcamps around the world. You must be 16 to go on a UK workcamp and 18 or over to go on an overseas workcamp.

- *Millennium Volunteers* – a government scheme to encourage young people (whether in work or unemployed) to do at least 200 hours of voluntary work in a twelve-month period.

- *Prince's Trust Volunteers* – teams of volunteers work on community projects for a sustained period.

- *The National Youth Agency* – publishes a free guide about full-time residential placements in Britain.

- *Volunteer bureaux* – located in towns throughout the country – the number of opportunities available ranges from dozens to hundreds, depending on the size of the local population.

- *Worldwide Volunteering for Young People* – has a computer database of over 800 organisations working on 250,000 projects in 200 countries. Matches young people aged 16 to 25 with suitable volunteering opportunities.

CASE STUDIES

Martin Houghton, social worker

'I started doing voluntary work before I left school. I served teas and dug gardens for old people – that kind of stuff. That was for Age Concern. Then I helped out with a local Riding for the Disabled group (I even learned to ride).

'After I left school I trained to be a baker, but after a year in the job I knew it wasn't for me, I missed working with people. So I applied to work as a care assistant in a home for people with severe learning difficulties and my volunteering meant I had the edge at interviews. It just grew from there and now I'm a social worker doing crisis intervention work. I'd probably be a bored baker if I hadn't done that volunteer work.'

Kay Sands, grants officer, large charitable trust, London

'I knew from early on that I wanted to work in the charity world so when I was at university I got heavily involved in the student Rag committee. We raised thousands of pounds each year for local charities. One of those charities knew about my work on the committee and asked me to join their committee to set up a membership organisation. I did it as a volunteer and then, when I left university, they offered me a six-month contract to work with its fund raising officer. That gave me the experience I needed to get a foot in the door here.'

Helen Kyriacos, student

'I want a job in marketing or sales when I leave university. I'm doing a business studies degree and it's great. But I also wanted to get some experience that would be a bit different, be fun and be challenging. I also wanted to earn some money.

So I collect money for charity. But not by rattling a can. I ask people to fill in donation forms to make regular donations. It really draws on my communication skills because I have to approach people, make contact and interest them in the charity. And then convince them to sign up to make regular donations. So I'm learning some great sales skills.

I don't work directly for the charity. Instead I work for a fundraising consultancy (you can find them on the Internet) and they do all the training and everything. The only downside is being out in the cold weather, but even that can be okay because you work in teams. There's always someone else on the same patch to talk to'.

CHECKLIST

◆ How can working in the voluntary sector boost your career prospects?

◆ When can you take your gap year?

♦ In what ways is working in the voluntary sector as much a real job as any other?

USEFUL RESOURCES

Useful addresses

BUNAC, 16 Bowling Green Lane, London EC1R 0BD.
Tel: (020) 7251 3472. www.bunac.org
E-mail: enquiries@bunac.org.uk

CSV (Community Service Volunteers), 237 Pentonville Road, London N1 9NJ. Tel: (020) 7278 6601. www.csv.org.uk E-mail: information@csv.org.uk

Gap Activity Projects (GAP) Ltd, GAP House, 44 Queen's Road, Reading, Berkshire RG1 4BB.
Tel: (0118) 959 4914. www.gap.org.uk
E-mail: volunteer@gap.org.uk

IVS (International Voluntary Service), Old Hall, East Bergholt, Nr Colchester CO7 6TQ. Tel: (01206) 298215. www.ivs-gb.org.uk
E-mail:ivssouth@ivs-gb.org.uk

Youth Volunteering Team, DfES, Room E4c, Moorfoot, Sheffield S1 4PQ. www.millenniumvolunteers.gov.uk
E-mail: millennium.volunteers@dfes.gsi.gov.uk

Prince's Trust, 18 Park Square East, London NW1 4LH.
Tel: (020) 7543 1200/freephone 0800 842842.
www.princes-trust.org.uk
E-mail: webinfops@princes-trust.org.uk

The National Youth Agency, Eastgate House, 19–23 Humberstone Road, Leicester LE5 3GJ. Tel: (0116) 242 7350.
www.nya.org.uk E-mail: nya@nya.org.uk

Students Partnership Worldwide, 17 Dean's Yard, London SW1P 3PB. Tel: (020) 7222 0138. www.spw.org

Email: spwuk@gn.upc.org Opportnities to live and work in partnership with local volunteers in Africa and Asia on health or environment projects.

Volunteer bureaux – the address of your nearest will be in the telephone directory.

Worldwide Volunteering for Young People. www.world-widevolunteering.org.uk An online searchable database of hundreds of thousands of volunteer opportunities.

Further reading

Before You Go, The Ultimate Guide To Planning Your Gap Year, Tom Griffiths (Bloomsbury, 2003).

The Gap Year Guidebook, 2005/06 (Peridot Press, 2005).

Planning Your Gap Year, 7th edition, Nick Vandome (How To Books, 2005).

Worldwide Volunteering, 4th edition (How To Books, 2004).

Surfing the Internet

YouthNet UK has a website called 'The Site' with information on volunteering and lots, lots more: www.thesite.org.uk

5

Giving Your Free Time

EXPLORING DIFFERENT WAYS OF VOLUNTEERING

Around 25 million people do some voluntary activity every year and about half of them are adults. About three-quarters are involved in fundraising activities (anything from doing a sponsored walk to working in a charity shop) and about a quarter are involved with voluntary sector organisations that are connected with sports, leisure and exercise.

One of the good things about volunteering is the amount of choice you have, not only in terms of what you do, but when, where and how you do it:

During the day – just about anything you can think of, from office and shop work to environmental research and car mechanics.

At night – on soup runs, telephone support lines, rescue organisations, hostels and refuges. If you're working during the day you can still give your time in the evening or during the night.

Part-time – from an hour a week upwards.

Full-time – this is normal if it's residential or overseas work that you are doing.

On a casual basis – this is fairly common with fundraising activities where you offer your time for a particular event.

On a regular basis – in terms of acquiring skills, understanding issues and making new friends, regular volunteering (anything upwards of once a week for the same organisation) is likely to be more rewarding. Also, many organisations couldn't provide the services they do unless people committed themselves to giving their time on a regular basis.

Locally – with so many voluntary sector organisations in the UK it's fair to say that there should be something you can do as a volunteer within walking distance of your home (certainly within a bus ride).

Away from home (including overseas) – this needs more planning, but it can be a great way to spend a holiday. The activities are, on the whole, likely to be more practical than administrative/clerical in nature.

Residential – if you are working with an organisation away from your home for more than one day it's normal for the organisation to arrange some sort of accommodation; this could be anything from a tent to the floor of a school hall to living with another family.

Indoors – working in offices, shops, workshops, studios, classrooms, hospitals, people's own homes – wherever there's a building.

Outdoors – anything from taking people on shopping trips to doing a survey of the local bat population.

At a manual level (skilled or unskilled) – if you have a skill like pottery or car mechanics you could teach it to others; you could learn a skill (such as gardening, cooking, decorating) through volunteering; or you could do manual work such as furniture collections or crop harvesting. There's also a lot of mundane and repetitive work to be done, like stuffing envelopes.

At an 'administrative' or 'leadership' level – perhaps running a shop or working in an office; being a team leader on a residential project or an expedition.

At a management level – on committees running organisations or projects.

The nature of the organisation you work with and for is up to you. It could be technical work, social, health, environmental, leisure, creative, religious, welfare (animal or human), campaigning – there really is a vast choice. See the section on volunteering in Chapter 2 for more ideas.

Getting paid for volunteering

Volunteering is nowadays quite complex and less easy to define than it used to be. For example, you can get paid for volunteering, both in the UK and overseas.

In the UK it is fairly common to be paid for voluntary positions that are residential and involve some type of care work, or for roles that have some element of leadership attached to them (for example, on conservation projects). If you are unemployed this can affect your social security rights and you should ask for detailed information from your Employment Service adviser before doing such voluntary work. (See the section below entitled 'The cons'.)

Some overseas positions are clearly voluntary and you will have to pay your own way; others will provide you with food and accommodation; yet others will pay you a 'salary'. Those that pay salaries try not to describe the people who do the work as volunteers – instead they use terms like 'development worker' – and they are often highly skilled professionals such as teachers and engineers. However, they are still often thought of as volunteer positions. Salaries are not as high as in the UK and the people who do the work give up a lot in order to do so and don't expect great rewards – in other words, the volunteer ethos is quite a strong factor in their motivation. See Chapter 8 for more information about these kinds of position.

Volunteering with public and private sector organisations

Although this book is about the voluntary sector, it is worth taking a brief look at other opportunities for volunteering.

In the public sector there are many opportunities to volunteer and there will be many similarities to volunteering in the voluntary sector. Among other things you could:

- ◆ be a Special Constable
- ◆ be a part-time fire-fighter
- ◆ be an auxiliary coastguard

- be a Justice of the Peace
- be a school governor
- volunteer with your local social services department.

In the private sector, companies sometimes take people on as volunteers so that the person can gain work experience. It is usually called 'unpaid work experience' rather than 'volunteering'. A good example is the media (newspapers, TV, publishing) where people do unpaid work experience in order to get a foot in the door or to get the necessary experience to get on a training course.

ASSESSING THE PROS AND CONS OF VOLUNTEERING

Volunteering can be very rewarding if you are clear about why you are doing it and about what you want to do (see Chapter 2). A lot of people feel that it's wrong to get something out of volunteering for themselves; they think it should be purely 'giving'. However, if you don't acknowledge that you will get something from it, you could end up feeling quite upset if, for example, someone you are trying to help rejects your 'gift' of help.

So before deciding to volunteer consider the following pros and cons:

The pros

- *Work experience* – you can gain valuable experience that could help to get you on a course of study or could improve your CV. For example, if you apply to do a physiotherapy course, any evidence of voluntary care work that you have done will be taken into account when you make your application.

- *Permanent work* – being a volunteer can lead to getting a permanent paid position in an organisation; being there as a volunteer gives you advantages like knowing when a job is coming up, understanding the issues and, of course, relevant work experience.

- *Skills and knowledge* – whatever you do it is likely that you will learn something new. For some types of voluntary work proper training is provided because the work is something you wouldn't be able to do without it. For example, some conservation organisations train people in things like dry stone walling or coppicing; if you want to be a counsellor the training provided is likely to lead to a qualification; working in a shop could provide you with basic personnel and retailing skills.

- *Test out job ideas* – if you are thinking of a career change or you are deciding which course to do at college, it could be useful to do some voluntary work that gives you an insight into what you might find in that kind of work or course. For example, if you are thinking of becoming a chef it might be a good idea to see if you can do some voluntary work in the kitchens of a homeless people's refuge.

- *Self-esteem* – it's important to recognise that at the very least being a volunteer is a chance to feel good about yourself. You might think of this in terms of feeling appreciated. If you feel you are not appreciated by the voluntary organisation you are with, there is nothing wrong with moving on; staying in the wrong place would be demotivating.

◆ *Friends* – volunteering can be a good way of finding new friends who share a common interest or outlook on life. This can be useful, for example, if you are moving to a new job in a different part of the country or if you have retired.

◆ *Networking* – networking is about making contacts with people and it is something we do all the time to a greater or lesser degree. It's a two-way process and is really about being aware of what other people are doing and letting them know what you are doing.

◆ *Travel* – some volunteer activities are available only in certain parts of the world and part of the reason for doing them is to travel and see those other places. Volunteering can be a great way of seeing different places and learning about different cultures.

◆ *Adventure* – you don't have to travel to have adventures and volunteering can be a way of seeing and exploring the world around you in a different way. Many volunteers have said how the volunteering they did changed their outlook on life.

◆ *Personal development* – as well as skills and knowledge and contacts, volunteering can give you a real sense of personal development. This can come from the kind of work you do, the kind of organisation you are working for or the kind of environment you are working in. There are lots of challenges to be faced in the voluntary sector and you can develop a depth of 'skills' such as flexibility, compassion, patience, communication, team-working, decision-making, confidence.

The cons

- *Pay* – as a volunteer you will get no pay or at least very little. For some jobs with some organisations you might get a contribution to your expenses, but for most volunteer positions you should not expect any financial reward. If you are thinking about volunteering overseas you may even have to pay to do it.

- *Monotony* – some volunteer work can be boring and repetitive with little contact with the people whom the organisation is helping. For example, can you stay motivated stuffing thousands of envelopes in an office when the work of the organisation is in overseas development, so you never actually see what's happening?

- *Commitment* – some organisations will ask you to commit yourself to work at certain times or for a certain period. This is especially common with organisations that provide structured training.

- *Cheap labour* – this is an issue to be aware of concerning your own voluntary position – you may be used as cheap labour. However, some organisations are very clear on this and have policies about not using volunteers where they can afford to pay for someone, or where the volunteer could be taking a paid worker's place.

- *Benefit sanctions* – if you are using volunteering as a way of building skills and experience to return to paid work, you need to check if your benefit entitlement will be affected. If you are claiming Jobseeker's Allowance you can do any number of hours' voluntary work each week, provided you are actively looking for paid work and can start a paid job within 48 hours. If you are getting pay, expenses or training that leads to a recognised qualification there is a chance that your benefits will be affected. It is important that you get the most up-to-date information you can. Your local volunteer bureau, Job Centre or Benefits Agency office (listed in the phone book) should be able to help you.

FINDING A VOLUNTEER POSITION

Once you know what you want to do and know what skills you have to offer, finding a volunteer position should be quite easy. There are certainly lots of different ways to go about it. You can find addresses and telephone numbers in this book, in telephone directories and in directories of voluntary work available at your reference library.

Making contact

Going to volunteer bureaux/shops
This is a useful general approach. Most large towns have volunteer bureaux and some smaller towns and even villages have a volunteer 'shop', which is open for a few hours each week. You can usually pop in and see one of the staff to discuss what volunteering opportunities are available. But it's a good idea to ring first because volunteer bureaux aren't always open all day and you might get seen more quickly if you can make an appointment.

Making a telephone call
If you know which organisation you want to work for (or at least what type of organisation) you can phone them up and ask about volunteer opportunities. Ask to speak to the volunteer co-ordinator (the job will be called different things in different organisations, but this should get you to the

right person). Ask about what opportunities there are for volunteering and ask how you can get involved. They may send you an information pack, give you the name of another volunteer to contact, or ask you to come in for a chat.

Writing a letter

If you decide to write to an organisation, keep your letter very brief. All you want at this stage is to find out if the organisation needs volunteers and if so how to become one. Don't include an SAE unless you have seen information about the organisation that instructs you to. Instead it's better to enclose a couple of first class stamps. See Figure 10 for an example of a letter asking for information.

Knocking on doors

Only do this if you are sure the organisation doesn't mind having unexpected visitors. A large organisation with large offices and a reception area may not mind, but small organisations with few staff may not have the resources to deal with people coming in off the street. Another disadvantage to 'cold calling' is that you might not get to see the most appropriate person – they could be off work or in a meeting. Having said that, you could get a small peek at how the organisation works and you could be in just the right place at just the right time.

Networking

If you know someone else who's a volunteer for the organisation you are interested in, quiz them for all the information you can about what the volunteers do, how to get involved and who to contact. Tell people you meet, even the person on the bus that you talk to, that you are interested in doing some voluntary work. You never know

1 My Street
The Town
Anywhere
A1 2B

02 July 200X

The Volunteer Coordinator
National Help Organisation
The City
Somewhere
Z2 6Y

Dear Volunteer Coordinator

Please send me information on becoming a volunteer with your organisation.

I enclose two first class stamps to cover postage.

Thank you.

Yours sincerely

Jones Smith

Even large voluntary sector organisations are run on tight budgets. They can receive hundreds of letters and telephone calls a day – all with offers of help. You can write a long letter if you want, but the chances are you will get no more information than the one above will. Remember that the point is to gather information efficiently – so keep it short.

Fig. 10. Sample letter, requesting information on volunteering.

what opportunities other people know about unless you talk to them.

Keeping your eyes and ears open
A lot of volunteer opportunities are advertised on leaflets or posters that you will see anywhere from your local library to the gates of a nearby country park. Some opportunities are announced on local radio. Others are advertised in newspapers, from local free sheets to *The Guardian*. *The Guardian* has a fortnightly volunteering page on Wednesdays.

Don't just look out for adverts, there are often small features in local papers and on local radio about how someone has raised money for a charity or how a community group is starting a new project. These are useful leads for finding the volunteer position you want.

For any voluntary position you may have to fill in an application form and/or have an interview. If this is the case see Chapter 3 for some useful ideas.

If you are applying to work as a volunteer with groups of people who could be classed as vulnerable (for example, children, the elderly, people with learning difficulties) it is possible that the organisation will want to run a criminal records check on you. See Chapter 6 for more information on this.

Asking some questions
When you contact an organisation, as well as being clear about what you want to do you should also have a few questions to ask of them:

- Is there an application process?
- How are volunteers selected?
- Is there a volunteer 'job description'?
- Is the organisation insured for its volunteers?
- What training does the organisation provide?

Of course, if you are interested in volunteering just for fun you may not be bothered about a 'job description', but you should always be clear about the organisation's insurance cover.

SERVING ON A COMMITTEE

There are two main types of committee in the voluntary sector:

1. **Management committees** – also called **Boards of Trustees** – they are legally responsible for the running of the organisation, though they do not necessarily have a day-to-day role.

2. **Project committees** – often known as steering groups, interest groups, working groups, committees or subcommittees – they are set up to get a project under way and to monitor it as it is implemented. If the project is to set up another organisation, the project committee may develop into a management committee once that organisation is set up.

People from all walks of life are on committees. The common element on any particular committee is that all the members are committed to the values and aims of the organisation. Working on a committee is a chance to use your specialist knowledge or skills. That knowledge may come from having worked in the sector for a number of years, or it may come from involvement in other ways. On the other hand, the skills you use on a committee may be the same ones you use in your job – if you are the treasurer you will need financial skills.

Committee work can be very exciting, as it is where policy matters are discussed and approved. Also committee members often have the chance to visit projects the organisation is involved in and attend review meetings with the organisation's staff. However, they do also have to discuss and review the minutiae of things like staff terms and conditions and make themselves familiar with the rules and regulations affecting the voluntary sector.

Getting on a committee

A lot of people who serve on committees are invited to do so by other members when a vacancy occurs. This is where the ability to network gives you an advantage – if people are aware of you, your skills, your commitment and your desire to serve on a committee, then they may think of you first.

However, it is also possible to register your interest in being a committee member. One way is to treat it as any other voluntary position and contact the charities you are interested in, explaining your interest and asking for further information. Another way is to register with CF Appointments (see Chapter 3).

Some organisations advertise when they want committee

members, but this isn't the normal method of recruiting, so if you decide to wait until the right organisation advertises you could wait a very long time.

Working on a committee

Committee work is basically management work, so you will be dealing with issues at a policy and planning level. It can be very rewarding because you will have a say in the direction and scope of the organisation's work. However, it is also a highly responsible position to be in and you will need clarity of thought and excellent interpersonal skills, including the ability to handle differences of opinion, to negotiate and to persuade.

Understanding your obligations

The details will vary from one organisation to another, but broadly speaking you can expect:

◆ To attend several meetings a year (anything from four upwards).

◆ To familiarise yourself with the organisation's work (through reading, visiting projects, meeting staff).

◆ To take on a special role (such as chairperson or, on a more ad hoc basis, responsibility for particular projects).

Being on a charity committee

Because charities are legally defined they are subject to much tighter controls than volunteer bodies and this also applies to the 'trustees' (the management committee members). As a trustee you:

- Must be over the age of 18.

- Have a legal responsibility for running the charity properly – including managing and protecting the property of the charity.

- Can be held legally responsible for the actions of the charity – this is why most charities are also limited companies, so that the financial risks to the trustees are limited.

- Can be paid reasonable expenses, but not a fee or salary for your services.

UNDERSTANDING WHAT YOU GET OUT OF IT

Provided you approach volunteer work in the right frame of mind you will undoubtedly benefit from it in some way. However, it is important to be realistic about the benefits and remember that it is how you make use of your experience that will make a difference to your life. You may feel after some voluntary experience that none of the pros mentioned above materialised for you. For example, you may have done some voluntary teaching work and found it boring or even hated it. However, you should be able to extract something positive from the experience. For example, did you try it to put something on your CV so you could do a teaching course? You still have something for your CV and you may now be clearer about whether teaching is the right career for you.

CASE STUDIES

Colleen Furney, business lecturer and charity trustee

'I lecture in business studies at university. One day a local charity contacted me looking for someone who could do some consultancy work on their strategic plans. Over the next three years I did various small consultancy projects (for which I was paid) for them. I suppose I just became more interested in their work and the issues facing them; I also met lots of the people involved with the management. I let the Director of the charity know I was interested in becoming a trustee. When a position on the board was vacated I was invited to become a member. I've now been a trustee for two years and even though it means I can't do any more consultancy work for them – I can't be paid for what I do – I feel I'm much more at the heart of things, not just a visitor.'

Sailesh Patel, Samaritans volunteer

'I've always been interested in personal development stuff – assertiveness, communication skills and things like that. The Samaritans thing just developed from that. It's not an easy thing to do – listening to someone who really might do what they say they're going to do – kill themselves. It's up and down emotionally and it can be quite draining. Since starting with the Samaritans and doing their training I've done a counselling certificate course and I'm looking at what else I can do. There's a need for counsellors in the Asian community and I want, eventually, to do some work in that line.'

Don Fletcher, retired

'I live in a small village and there's not much in the way of facilities for young people. One day I was reading the local free-sheet and I read about the local youth football team facing a shutdown because there was no one to coach them. I'd played for the works team before retiring and I'd even coached them for a couple of seasons when I was too old to play. So I got in touch with the club to see if I could be of any help, and they said to come down. As it turned out, two others turned up as well – John, who's retired, and Mick. But we got on so well we thought we'd give it a go with all of us sharing the coaching. I'm not saying we never disagree, but it's working really well and it's great to get out in the fresh air and have a bit of exercise.'

Barbara Doyle, early retired

'I took early retirement a couple of years ago when the company was reducing the workforce. I got a really good deal, which means I can now work part time. But before I got another job I wanted to do something different. I'd done some travelling when I was younger and I really felt it was a good time to go again as the children are grown up and I'm divorced.

I suppose you could say I took a gap year. I did a lot of research on the Internet and in the library, especially about things like inoculations and security. Doing all that research made me realise there's not a lot to worry about really. If you prepare well and you are open to learn from others you can't go far wrong.

I ended up spending six months in Africa and six months in Asia. In Africa I worked on a health project and in Asia I worked on a conservation project. I went with different organisations so I had to be very good with all the paperwork, not to get it mixed up.

But I wouldn't have missed it for anything. I made new

friends, young and old. I saw some amazing parts of the world. And I feel more confident that I did when I finished work – I have something interesting to talk about and I have an opinion about things that comes from experience. It's great.'

CHECKLIST

- How many different ways can you become a volunteer?
- What are the pros and cons of volunteering?
- What are the different ways to find a volunteer position?
- What are the special obligations of committee work?

USEFUL RESOURCES

Watch out for **Volunteers Week** (www.volunteersweek.org.uk) – an annual event that aims to raise the profile of volunteering in the UK. It usually runs in the summer and during the week there will be lots of information available and activities going on in your local area, making volunteering a lot more visible. It's co-ordinated by the agencies listed below under 'Useful addresses'.

Useful addresses

Volunteering Development Agency, 4th floor, 58 Howard Street, Belfast BT1 6PG. Tel: (02890) 236 100.
www.volunteering-ni.org
Email: info@volunteering-ni.org.

Volunteering England, Regent's Wharf, 8 All Saints Street, London N1 9RL. Tel: (020) 7520 8901.
E-mail: volunteersweek@volunteeringengland.org.uk

Volunteer Development Scotland, Stirling Enterprise Park, Stirling FK7 7RP. Tel: (01786) 479593.
www.vds.org.uk. E-mail: information@vds.org.uk

Wales Council for Voluntary Action, Baltic House, Mount Stuart Square, Cardiff Bay, Cardiff CF10 5FH. Tel: (02920) 431 700. www.wcva.org.uk E-mail: enquiries@wcva.org.uk

Further reading

The Voluntary Agencies Directory 2004 (National Council for Voluntary Organisations). The directory is published every two years. It contains information on over 2,500 voluntary organisations. However, it is expensive – rather than buying it, see if your local reference library has a copy.

6

Making a Career in the Voluntary Sector

FINDING A PAID POSITION

The voluntary sector is not short of opportunities for the paid worker. A rough estimate would put the figure of paid positions at somewhere over half a million. Add to this the fact that there are many young, mobile people working in the sector and that quite a few jobs are project based (lasting for only the life of the project) and you will get some sense of the number of jobs available at any one time.

There is paid work to be done at all levels, dealing with all kinds of issues (from fighting racism in football to promoting leisure and education for the elderly). Also it is possible to work almost anywhere in the country (or even the world). Just as with voluntary work it would be surprising if you were unable to find something you are interested in.

Looking for a job

When you are looking for a job you need to be focused – which is about knowing what you want to do and why, and using every resource available to you. Use the agencies, resources and ideas discussed in Chapter 5, but bear in mind that (apart from networking – which is productive if unpredictable) there are basically three ways of finding paid work:

1. trawling through job pages
2. registering with recruitment agencies
3. making speculative applications.

Trawling through job pages
Paid jobs in the voluntary sector are advertised in the media just like other jobs, though it's useful to know where to start.

As far as newspapers are concerned, your local one is always worth looking at. Even the national voluntary sector organisations advertise jobs locally if they have a local office.

The best national newspaper for voluntary sector careers is *The Guardian* where jobs in this sector are advertised every Wednesday. *The Observer* has some voluntary sector appointments on the Work pages of its Business section.

If you are looking for overseas work you will find jobs advertised in all these publications though if you have a Teletext service or access to the Internet, it is worth checking on the jobs pages or searching the websites of individual organisations.

Registering with recruitment agencies
It is always worth trying places like the Job Centre or high street recruitment consultants, though there are a few dedicated voluntary sector recruitment agencies (see Chapter 3). There are also recruitment 'agencies', such as *monster*, on the Internet. These are places where you can search through masses of jobs by type, region, sector, pay

level and so on until you find what you want. You can also post your CV on some of these sites so that employers can look for you.

Making speculative applications

It is always worth considering making a speculative application, particularly if your field of knowledge and experience is very specialised, very sought after or both. Generally voluntary sector organisations have stringent equal opportunities policies, which mean speculative applications aren't favoured. However, it's always possible you will be put on file, or better still a mailing list, and asked to make an application when a job does come up.

Speculative applications can work well if you are applying to work overseas. Organisations like VSO, for example, have 'registers' of people wanting to work in developing countries. The disadvantage of such an approach is that it can be months before anything suitable comes up.

If you do take this approach either find out (by phoning) to whom applications should be addressed, or address your application to the personnel manager. That way it will get to the right person even if the organisation is too small to have a personnel manager. Don't write to the Director or the Chair because your application may end up being sidelined or delayed by internal channels.

Knowing when to look for jobs

As far as local papers are concerned, you need to find out when the best day for jobs is. Most papers have certain days when there will be more of one type of advertisement than another (for example, houses on Saturday, cars on

Friday, jobs on Thursday). For *The Guardian* the best day is Wednesday, followed by Monday and Saturday; *The Observer*, of course, is on Sunday.

For other sources such as agencies, Teletext and the Internet it's probably worth registering where you can and checking to see if there's any progress on a regular basis.

As far as seasons of the year go, you may have noticed that there are fewer jobs (whatever the sector) advertised in the papers in December, January, July and August. This is simply because these are not cost-effective times to advertise. Potential applicants are too busy doing other things – preparing for Christmas, settling back to work, going on holiday, changing their car – and organisations find selections more difficult to organise because of internal pressures of staff taking time off for holidays. So, there won't be as many jobs advertised at these times of the year. But it's still important to keep looking because it could be then that you find a job – and if there aren't as many people looking there could be less competition.

Working overseas
Finding paid work overseas (at a rate equivalent to UK pay) is more difficult than finding it in the UK. Firstly, there are far fewer opportunities – a lot of organisations that work in developing countries now employ local people to run their overseas offices. Secondly, the person specification will usually require that you have previous overseas work experience (usually gained as a volunteer) of

around two years. See Chapter 8 for more information on working abroad.

EXPLORING WHAT JOBS ARE AVAILABLE

Sampling a few areas

To get an idea of the range of jobs available in the voluntary sector take a look at the lists in Chapters 1 and 2. Also, look through the jobs pages of *The Guardian* on any Wednesday.

If you feel you don't have any 'specialist' skills, remember that whatever work an organisation does – whether it's replanting woodland areas or building accommodation for the disabled – it will need an office of some sort to run the 'business' side of things. So, even if you are a committed conservationist, but without practical conservation skills, you may find the right role for you in the office of a conservation organisation.

However, if you have specific skills (and voluntary experience) your chances of finding the job you want at the level you want will be much improved.

You can sample work experience in the voluntary sector by doing the Foundation Course run by Working for a Charity. This consists of seven full-day workshops spread over several weeks and a supervised work placement in a voluntary sector organisation for a minimum of 20 days. On the application form you can specify the type of work you are best suited to do and the type of organisation you would like to work for. Placements can often be arranged in your own area.

UNDERSTANDING JOB DESCRIPTIONS AND PERSON SPECIFICATIONS

When you receive information about a job from a voluntary sector organisation there should be at least a job description. Sometimes there will also be a person specification telling you what qualifications, skills, experience and personal qualities are needed to do the job. Understanding these documents will help you make a decision about whether to apply and will also help you to make a better application.

Decoding job descriptions

Every job description is different, so decoding it is really a matter of asking some questions and thinking about the implications of the answers.

- How is it presented?
- How many duties and responsibilities are there on it?
- Does it tell you if there is any supervisory responsibility?
- Does it tell you the purpose of the post?
- Does it make clear any special conditions?

Presentation

A well laid-out job description with clear headings and decent-sized type is your first indication that the organisation has put some thought into the recruitment process. A poorly laid-out description doesn't necessarily indicate the contrary, but it should put you on the lookout for other indicators (poor telephone manner when you ring, your interview running unreasonably late or over time).

Length

A good job description will be no more than two or three pages long, though physical length is relative to the presentation. The real issue is how many duties and responsibilities are on the description, and how much detail there is on each item. A job description is really a template – it should allow for the fact that no two people can do the same job in exactly the same way. An overly detailed job description might indicate a heavily bureaucratic organisation or that there is more than one job to be done.

On the other hand, a job description with only one or two duties on it might tell you that the organisation either doesn't really need this post, or hasn't considered how it fits in with the rest of the organisation.

Supervision

A good job description will indicate whom you will answer to and who will answer to you. If you have to answer equally to several people you could find yourself in some delicate situations in which you will need to develop some excellent diplomatic skills. If a job description does not indicate supervision you will need to find this out.

Purpose

This is a general statement about why the post is necessary. Again, it should be brief and with not too many points. A good job description will have between one and four purposes and you should be able to see a common thread running through them. If there are lots of purposes and they seem at odds with each other, you need to question how many jobs the organisation is really asking you to do.

Special conditions

This is a general area where you should find information about any travel, unsocial hours, significant pressures and other conditions of the work. If there is no information about these kinds of issues it doesn't mean they aren't present in the job, so you need to be ready to ask about them at interview.

Decoding person specifications

A person specification tells you what skills, qualifications and experience you should have to do the job. A really good person specification will tell you at what stage the recruitment team will be looking for them – on your application form, during interview, or during assessment exercises.

Again, presentation is important because this is a document that should be easy to read and understand. At the very least it should split the requirements into 'essential' and 'desirable' categories.

If something appears under the heading of 'essential' this means that it is no use applying for that job unless you have that particular skill, experience or qualification. Even if there are ten essentials and you have nine of them you may be wasting your time by applying. However, if you have all of the essentials and none of the desirables, it could still be worth sending in your application. Things under 'desirable' are those that an organisation believes will enhance a person's ability to do a job, rather than being vital.

See Figure 11 for an example of a person specification.

THE NATIONAL AUTISTIC SOCIETY

EMPLOYEE SPECIFICATION
PROJECT OFFICER – CHESHIRE
(Families & Services)
(Up to 2 ½ years contract)

The essential and desirable characteristics of the post leader are indicated by "X".

CATEGORY	ESSENTIAL	DESIRABLE
A. Qualifications		
Recognised Social Work qualification eg. Dip SW, CQSW, CSS or equivalent	X	
B. Knowledge		
Autism	X	
Knowledge of legislation relating to children and care	X	
Awareness of local services and resources to be made available to individuals with autism	X	
Knowledge of range of services available to meet individual needs	X	
C. Skills		
Entrepreneurial skills	X	
Development and organisation skills	X	
Excellent interpersonal skills	X	
Ability to manage own workload	X	
D. Work Experience		
Minimum three years experience in a management position in services for people with disabilities	X	
Working with children or adults with autism	X	

User16: Jobdes\Project.che

Fig. 11. Sample person specification – National Autistic Society.

THE NATIONAL AUTISTIC SOCIETY

EMPLOYEE SPECIFICATION
PROJECT OFFICER – CHESHIRE
(Families & Services)
(Up to 2½ years contract)

CATEGORY	ESSENTIAL	DESIRABLE
D. Work Experience		
Experience of working with people with challenging behaviour	X	
Formulating policies and procedures relating to good care practice	X	
Involved in developing and working with individual programmes	X	
Supervision of staff/volunteers		X
Advocacy		X
Reviewing service provision/developing new services		X
E. Personal Qualities		
Self motivation/ability to work on own initiative	X	
Ability to make decisions	X	
Ability to advocate	X	
Tact and diplomacy	X	
Confidentiality	X	
Commitment to Equal Opportunities	X	
Commitment to NVQ (via PII)	X	
Commitment to ongoing personal training and development	X	

User16: Jobdes\Project.che

Fig. 11. (continued).

UNDERSTANDING TERMS AND CONDITIONS

You may be sent information about terms and conditions with information about the job you are applying for. In the voluntary sector generally there is a concern for equal opportunities so, unlike the private sector, individual negotiation around such matters is unlikely.

Pay

It should be clear when you will be paid, what salary scale you will be on and when increments will be due. It should also be clear whether you will be paid or get time-off-in-lieu (TOIL) for any overtime. Many voluntary sector organisations do not pay for overtime, but instead operate a TOIL system. It should be clear how this works.

Holidays

Holidays in the voluntary sector vary. Some are very good and offer 25 days annual leave plus bank holidays. Some organisations offer fewer days, but follow the public sector practice of giving two days leave for most of the bank holidays.

Maternity/paternity leave

Maternity leave is usually well provided for in the voluntary sector, but paternity leave is something that is not generally provided. If there is no information on this in the terms and conditions make sure you clarify the situation before accepting a job.

Relocation

It is unlikely that a small, local organisation would be in a position to offer relocation expenses. The relocation packages offered by larger organisations are generally for senior posts. Whatever the case, don't expect the same level of compensation as you would receive in the private sector.

Criminal records

If you are applying for a job working with vulnerable groups of people such as children, women or the elderly, the employing organisation may check to see whether you have a criminal record. This is to protect the people that the organisation supports. Further information about what you have to declare and what the organisation is allowed to check out for itself can be obtained from NACRO (National Association for the Care and Resettlement of Offenders).

Confidentiality

There may be a clause in your contract about confidentiality, especially with organisations such as rape crisis centres or refuges. Breaking confidentiality in such cases can merit instant dismissal because of the potentially terrible impact it can have on other people's lives, and because it can bring the organisation into disrepute.

Pensions

The voluntary sector is generally quite good at looking after its staff and pension cover may be provided on a contributory or non-contributory basis.

Smoking

Like everywhere else, many voluntary sector organisations now have no-smoking policies. This could mean that smoking is not allowed in the offices or public areas in an organisation's building. It could mean that smoking is not allowed anywhere on the organisation's property, including its land and vehicles (if it has any).

ASSESSING THE FINANCIAL REWARDS

Whatever the financial rewards of the kinds of job you are interested in, you need to measure them against your expectations, not just of money, but of your lifestyle.

Working in the UK

There are a lot of professional staff in the voluntary sector and their pay is at professional levels. However, it's important not to expect the same as you would get in the private sector.

Average salaries for chief executives of charities with annual incomes of around £3–10 million are around £46,000. The average for chief executives of commercial companies with the same turnover is almost twice as much (£80,000).

One of the best-paid areas in the voluntary sector is fundraising. Good fundraisers are highly sought after and well rewarded. The fundraising director of a £10–25 million charity can expect to earn around £40,000.

At the lower end (clerical assistant, receptionist, secretarial, and assistant officer type positions) jobs are quite well paid. They may be comparable with the private sector. For example, it's not unusual for secretaries to earn between £8,000 and £14,000.

But whatever the level you work at in the voluntary sector, there is an absence of the perks that you might find in commercial companies. For example, there are few jobs for which a company car is provided, and private health care insurance is unusual, as are bonuses and productivity incentives.

Working overseas

If you are working in a developing country with one of the 'volunteer' sending organisations (ICD, Skillshare International, VSO, etc.) you will receive a 'local' salary or allowance and it will seem very small from a UK perspective. Around £400 a month is not unusual. However, if you consider that this may be untaxed (or low-taxed), that at least a flight each way will be provided (and maybe a holiday flight in the middle of your contract), that your National Insurance will be paid, medical insurance provided, and rent-free accommodation and furnishings thrown in, it will enable you to live comfortably, although perhaps less so if you travel with your family.

If you are working as the direct employee of a UK organisation your salary could well be anywhere upwards of £14,000 and you could be getting all the other benefits that have just been mentioned. On the other hand, you may have to pay for your own accommodation, National Insurance and so on, and your salary may be taxed as soon as you return to the UK.

EXPLORING PROMOTION PROSPECTS AND JOB SECURITY

Job security and promotion prospects in the voluntary sector are to some extent dependent on the size of the organisation, the nature of its work, and whether its cause is 'fashionable'. And, of course, how ambitious you are.

Again, it is a matter of thinking about your long-term

career plans. If you want to work your way up in the voluntary sector it will demand a great deal of energy, flexibility and mobility (you may have to move to another location to get the results you want).

Job titles can be a hindrance where there is no equivalent from one organisation to another or in the private sector. A title such as Project Officer is more likely to be understood across sectors than Placement Officer or Field Co-ordinator, for example.

In small organisations straightforward promotions are not always possible so if you are regraded (i.e. put on a higher salary scale) it's a good opportunity to see if you can have your job title changed so that you can put this down on your CV as a promotion.

In order to get a promotion you may need particular experience, such as working in direct contact with a particular section of society (the homeless, drug users, prostitutes, for example). One of the best ways of getting this experience is by volunteering.

CASE STUDIES

John Tallins, ecologist, woodland conservation charity

'I think of myself as a scientist, first and foremost. But I'm lucky because my laboratory is outside. I plan surveys, organise volunteers to do them, do some of my own small-scale surveys, and analyse results. If we need any laboratory work doing I contract it out. The reports I write can have a big impact on the local area so I feel quite a bit of pressure to get things right. The money isn't brilliant and there are no perks apart from working outdoors a lot of the time. Having said that, last year I got to visit a project in India that's been a real success to see if there was anything we could learn from them.'

Francis Canon, manager, environmental charity

'I manage the communications services within the organisation. That means I'm responsible for looking at everything from how we do business with the Post Office to how our computers are networked. A project I'm working on now is to try to reduce the amount of paper we use in our offices – it makes sense for an organisation like us. It means getting people together to find out what and how they want to communicate and seeing how much we can do by computers or by changing the way we run our meetings and so on. I also manage two assistants and a large budget so I draw on a lot of skills in this job.'

Sarah Fielden, information officer, local drugs project

'I first got involved with the project as a volunteer. A friend overdosed on drugs and I just wanted to do something useful. I was managing a high street fashion store at the time and I just found the volunteer work was getting more interesting and I thought the stuff they were dealing with was fascinating. When this job came up I applied and got it. We're only a small organisation so I feel involved in everything. My own job is fairly broad anyway – I put together funding applications, write news releases, work on publicity campaigns and even visit local schools doing educational work. I'd like to go more into fundraising, but I'll have to move on to a bigger organisation to specialise.'

CHECKLIST

♦ What different ways are there of finding work?

♦ What questions should you consider when looking at a job description?

♦ What's the value of a person specification?

♦ What are the terms and conditions like, the salaries and the long-term prospects?

USEFUL RESOURCES

Useful addresses

NACRO, 169 Clapham Road, London SW9 0PU. Tel: (020) 7582 6500. NACRO produces a range of free leaflets with useful advice for ex-offenders. www.nacro.org.uk. E-mail: working@nacro.org.uk

Working for a Charity, NCVO, Regent's Wharf, 8 All Saints Street, London N1 9RL. Tel: (020) 7520 2512. www.wfac.org.uk Email: enquiries@wfac.org.uk

7

Moving Up, Moving On

WORKING IN THE VOLUNTARY SECTOR AS PART OF YOUR WIDER CAREER PLANS

Having worked through the other chapters of this book (especially Chapters 2 and 3) you should now have a reasonably clear idea of why you want to work in the voluntary sector. Once you are working in the sector, either as a volunteer or as a member of staff, it is likely at some stage that you will find yourself considering a number of questions:

◆ Could I do more?
◆ How could I do more?
◆ Where can I go now?
◆ What do I need to do in order to move on?

Moving up in the voluntary sector

Going from volunteering to paid work
Doing voluntary work is a useful way of getting a step on the ladder to a career in the voluntary sector. It helps you to understand the way the sector works, gives you contacts and helps you to build up relevant skills and experiences for getting paid work.

Going up the promotion ladder
Career development in the voluntary sector may seem less

'vertical' than in other sectors. In other words, career paths may be less clear, but there will be opportunities to take 'sideways' promotions and temporary responsibility for projects above your grade. Moving into areas outside your own speciality may be more normal. In 1998 the RSA (Royal Society of Arts) published a report about work in the voluntary sector, which described the career structure as 'spiral'.

What this means in practical terms for your career is that if you want to be a manager, the route to that position is less likely to be a straightforward one, than in the private sector. It is not simply a case of waiting for the position above you to become vacant and then applying for it, and so on, until you reach the position you want. Part of the problem with this approach is that many organisations are too small for this to be a fruitful tactic – staff turnover is either too slow or the difference in job levels is too great for internal promotion to be feasible.

On the other hand, having to move around in order to move up means that you could develop a wider under-standing of the issues that affect your work and that of the organisation. It's also an excellent way of developing a wider portfolio of skills.

Moving on to other sectors
If you are unemployed or looking for your first job after college, experience of voluntary work can show potential employers that you have initiative and a real desire to work (see Chapters 4 and 5).

If you are doing paid work in the voluntary sector it is important that you are able to show employers in other sectors that you have developed skills that will be useful to them. You also need to bear in mind that you will be competing with people who have more commercial experience than you, so you will need to show, from your CV onwards, that your experience is appropriate. For example, many advertisements for positions in the private sector are looking for people who can work under pressure and have experience of a competitive environment. You'll need to re-assess your voluntary sector experiences in the light of this and present them accordingly.

DEVELOPING YOUR SKILLS

While you are working in the voluntary sector it is important for your career development and for keeping up your interest that you continue to expand and develop your skills. Some skills you will develop by doing the work on a day-to-day basis. Others you may develop by going on courses, which may lead to qualifications.

The availability of training in the voluntary sector is variable. The organisation you work for may not be able to afford to pay for a training course, but they may be able to find other ways of supporting you through one. For example, if you are willing to pay for a course yourself, your employer may be willing to let you have a few hours each week of paid study time.

Doing a course

Many voluntary organisations provide their own training courses to meet their own needs. For example, one member of staff who can use a particular computer software package may be encouraged to train others how to use it. Or the organisation may develop its own training package (sometimes leading to a recognised qualification) that it can use with new staff and volunteers. This may be the case with organisations that provide counselling services or do conservation work, for example.

There are a number of organisations that provide courses tailored to the voluntary sector in general:

♦ **Charity People** provides access courses for people new to the voluntary sector; software package training; courses in communication skills, self-marketing and fundraising.

♦ **Directory of Social Change** provides training courses in management, supervision, personnel and training skills; personal development; communication; fundraising; and finance and law. The courses are available at different levels, from beginner to very experienced. Publishes a training course catalogue and a publications catalogue.

♦ **National Centre for Volunteering** provides training in all aspects relating to the management of volunteers. Publishes a training and publications catalogue.

♦ Various universities run distance-learning courses relevant to the voluntary sector that can lead to the Professional Certificates and Diplomas in Management with modules addressing management issues specifically in relation to the public and non-profit sectors.

Apart from these there are specific courses at all levels that will be relevant to your own work and interests. For example, if you are working on an inner city car project you might be thinking about college courses in mechanics or youth work. As with the public and private sectors, the general principle applied to providing training for individuals is to ask whether it is relevant to the work they are doing. If the organisation you are working for does not seem to be aware of what training is available, it may be worth going to your local careers advisory office. They will have information about all types of courses available locally.

Getting accreditation for your skills

Apart from doing courses that lead to qualifications, another way of getting a nationally recognised certificate for your skills is to do an NVQ (National Vocational Qualification).

The good thing about NVQs (SNVQs in Scotland) is that they don't depend on examinations. Getting a qualification depends on the work you are doing. In other words, if you're already doing the work, you might as well get a qualification for it. Of course, it's not as simple as just turning up to work every day and then getting a certificate. You have to prove that you are competent at certain things, and someone from outside your organisation assesses your work.

There are hundreds of NVQs available in a range of areas, including:

- animals, plants and land
- transport
- goods and services
- health, social and protective services
- business services
- communicating.

They start at Level 1, which is basic and shows your ability to do routine tasks, and go up to Level 5, which is intended to be equivalent to a postgraduate qualification and is suitable for senior managers. You don't have to start at Level 1 and work upwards – you can take the level most appropriate to the work you are doing.

The good thing about NVQs is that they are designed by employers and so are recognised throughout the country. They also provide you with a means of getting a qualification without having to take a career break.

Opportunities to do NVQs in the voluntary sector are variable, but most organisations see the benefit of them and some positively encourage them. Over 50 per cent of the NVQs awarded in Environmental Conservation are gained by BTCV (British Trust for Conservation Volunteers) volunteers.

Information about NVQs should be available from your local careers office.

UPDATING YOUR CV
It's a good idea to keep your CV on a word processor file if you can, so that it is easily adapted to suit different

employers and quickly updated. Even so it's worthwhile having at least two separate CVs:

1. Your 'base' CV – this is just a list which you can divide up into sections and then list everything chronologically. This way you won't forget a half-day training course that you did last year.

2. Your 'model' CV – this is your skeleton which has all the right shapes and components, but which you flesh out each time you apply for a job.

If your career is focused within the voluntary sector then your experiences in the sector will appear on your CV under 'work experience'. But if you are, or have been a volunteer, or your paid experience in the sector was a long time ago, you need to think about whether that experience is relevant to your current application and how best to present it on your CV. Updating your CV isn't just about putting new things on – it's also about deciding when to remove things, or reduce or change the emphasis on them.

Keep things brief and simple, and relevant to the job you are applying for. You will be putting more detail on your CV about your current or most recent job, so the further away in time a job is the less detailed and the more pertinent it will have to be.

If your experience in the voluntary sector is as a volunteer you will need to consider where to put this on your CV. If you were unemployed at the time and volunteered several days a week it's quite legitimate and very positive to put this down under 'work experience' provided you make it clear it was voluntary. On the other hand, if your volunteering has been on an ad hoc basis or something that you do in your spare time, you could either make a separate section for it on your CV (if it's significant enough) or put it under an 'other information' section.

If you are applying for a job in the private sector that needs experience of 'fast-moving, competitive' environments, don't forget that organisations in the voluntary sector are competing for resources (money, materials and help) and responding to pressures and crises all the time. It's simply a matter of re-interpreting your own experience to match the needs of the employer.

KEEPING IN TOUCH

Keeping in touch with the private sector

If you are working more or less full-time in the voluntary sector for a significant period (anything above three months) whether paid or unpaid, and you think you might return to the private sector, it is important to remain in contact.

- ◆ If, for example, you are on secondment or leave of absence, make sure that you stay in touch with your old colleagues by telephone, e-mail or letter – even the odd note on a greetings card. It will help you to keep in touch with what's going on and if and when you do return, it won't feel so strange.

- ◆ If you worked in a particular industry or profession (whether it's health or brewing) try to keep up any membership subscriptions you have and stay on the mailing list for newsletters and journals.

♦ At the very least keep an eye on the jobs pages of newspapers so that you can get an idea if jobs are changing or if entry requirements are getting tougher.

Keeping in touch with the voluntary sector

If you decide to stop doing paid work for a particular organisation or cause in the voluntary sector you may still want to help out occasionally and volunteering is one way of doing that. You could volunteer in one of the many ways mentioned in Chapter 5.

However, if you no longer want to volunteer you may still want to feel as though you are making a contribution in some way. You could do this by:

♦ *Becoming a non-active member* – paying your subscriptions and receiving newsletters.

♦ *Making regular donations* by direct debit or including an organisation in your will.

♦ *Becoming a freelance adviser or consultant* – using your experience within the sector to advise other organisations. This gives you the freedom to do other work while still being involved in the sector.

♦ *Staying in touch on a personal level* – this may be obvious if you have made good friends during your work, but even on a professional level it can be useful to have an extra contact for references.

CASE STUDIES

Anne-Marie Moore, administration officer, Skillshare International

'I left school at 16 and found a job with a company where I was doing an NVQ, but it didn't work because there was no support. Then Skillshare took me on as an admin trainee.

'I was hired on the basis I would go on to NVQ Level 3. I got my Business Administration Level 1 in six months and went on straight away to do Level 2. It was good because one of the other women here was going for her NVQ assessor's award, so she was able to use me as a case study and support me on an almost daily basis.

'After Level 2 I went on to do Level 3 and it took about 18 months to get all three levels. I could have gone down the secretarial qualification route, but I wanted to do the business administration. Doing the NVQs gave me more confidence and I'm now thinking about studying for higher education qualifications.'

Tony Markham, freelance photographer

'I really got into photography when I was an assistant in the fundraising unit of a local homelessness project. It was called the fundraising unit, but it did everything to do with publicity and marketing so there was always a lot of work going on with leaflets and exhibitions, and there was a lot of discussion about how we should have images of our clients that were positive, that didn't patronise them.

'Our stock of photographs was quite old and so someone decided it would be a good idea to buy a camera and get everyone – staff, volunteers, clients – to take pictures of the things that mattered to them about the project. It took quite a lot of organising and I got more and more involved until really I was running it as a little project in its own right. I suppose I must have done well because I was sent on photography courses.

'I thought there must be a market for this kind of skill with other groups so I started asking around and putting a portfolio together, until I'd done enough and felt confident enough to set up on my own. I think my background in the voluntary sector has definitely given me the edge in winning some commissions – I know what the issues are and why they matter.'

Jackie Nelson, finance officer, animal welfare organisation

'I've always worked in the voluntary sector and I've done all sorts of things. But I've always been interested in numbers and computers so whatever job I was doing I was looking for opportunities to develop skills in those areas – I suppose I've always been fairly ambitious.

'A few years ago I was in a project development team at a large charity and I was responsible for applying for grants from big donors like the European Union. When we got the money I had to monitor how it was spent and what the results were. My skills were developing fast because I would go on courses and then have to apply what I'd learnt to a real-life situation straight away.

'One of the courses I did was an OU management certificate course about finance and accounting. That was brilliant – it helped me get this job and it gave me confidence to study for accountancy qualifications by correspondence. The course is really expensive, but my employer pays and I repay them a little bit each month. They also let me have a half-day of study leave every week.'

CHECKLIST

◆ What kind of career pattern might you expect in the voluntary sector?

◆ How can you develop your skills while working in the voluntary sector?

◆ What are the two CVs you should have?

◆ What are the advantages of keeping in touch with the sector you have left behind?

USEFUL RESOURCES

Useful addresses

Charity People, 38 Bedford Place, Bloomsbury, London WC1B 5JH. Tel: (020) 7299 8700.
www.charitypeople.co.uk

Directory of Social Change, 24 Stephenson Way, London NW1 2DP. Tel: (020) 7391 4800. www.dsc.org.uk
E-mail: info@dsc.org.uk

National Centre for Volunteering, Regent's Wharf, 8 All Saints Street, London N1 9RL. Tel: (020) 7520 8900.
www.volunteering.org uk
E-mail: information@volunteeringengland.org.uk

HERO – Higher Education and Research Opportunities – a website providing a gateway to all universities and higher education colleges in the UK. www.hero.ac.uk

Centre for Educational Development, University of Wales, Lampeter, College Street, Lampeter, Ceredgion SA58 7ED. Tel: (01570) 424785. www.volstudy.ac.uk

Contact your local careers office for information about training courses and NVQs. You can find their address in the telephone book.

Further reading

CVs for High Flyers: Elevate Your Career with a CV that Gets You Noticed, Rachel Bishop-Firth (How To Books, 2004).

Write a Great CV, Paul McGee (How To Books, 2003).

(8)

Working Overseas

'Adventure' is a word that sums up a lot about working
overseas, especially when it is work done with voluntary
sector organisations. There seems to be a perception that
if you are working on a forestry project in Nepal it is
somehow closer to 'real life' than working on a
commercial farm in New Zealand. There's also a
perception that it's more adventurous because it isn't
cosseted – you get paid nothing or very little so you have
to live just like the local people, or sleep in tents in the
middle of nowhere.

While there is an element of truth in all of this, it is
important that you are realistic about what to expect and
this means doing some preparation.

FINDING OUT ABOUT DIFFERENT ORGANISATIONS
Before applying to an organisation it's a good idea to find
out what kind of work they are involved in, what kind of
people they are looking for and what kind of terms and
conditions you can expect.

There are excellent books and directories (see Useful
Resources at the end of this chapter) listing hundreds of
organisations and giving brief details about them. Use
these to make a shortlist of organisations you are
interested in and then contact them for more information.

The overseas work done by voluntary sector organisations can be split into two broad categories:

1. Development work.
2. Relief emergency work.

Development work has long-term aims, usually to do with empowering people and raising their standard of living. Relief or emergency work is often more of a short-term response to a crisis event such as drought, war or earthquake. Some organisations specialise in one type of work, but others do both.

Another split that can be made concerns the length of time that people might be asked to commit to working overseas:

1. Short-term work is usually anything from a week to a year.
2. Long-term work can be anything from six months to two years.

The longer the period of time that you want to spend overseas, the more likely it is that you will need specific job skills and qualifications. However, there are some organisations, such as RedR (Register of Engineers for Disaster Relief) which take only skilled people regardless of the length of placement.

If you want to go overseas with a partner or with your family you will need to find an organisation that supports this. Not all do. Some take only single people while others will accept partners, but not children. If you intend to take your family overseas it will be much more expensive and there will be more issues to consider, such as what will your partner do while you are at work, and will you be able to get schooling for your children?

Being on a register

If you are able to go overseas at short notice for brief periods you may be interested in registering with one of the organisations that responds to crisis situations. RedR is one, Oxfam and British Red Cross are others.

There are also registers for skilled people who are interested in longer-term work. Addresses of these can be found in the Useful Resources section at the end of this chapter.

PREPARING TO WORK ABROAD

On the one hand, it's important to do as much preparation as possible before going overseas. Once you are 6,000 miles away from home, sorting out that problem with the bank won't be very easy. On the other hand, you don't want to do so much preparation that you get bored and feel that the adventure is disappearing under a mountain of paperwork. So the thing to remember is to be organised and to pace yourself.

Making practical preparations

This is the part of your preparation that you must be very thorough about. It would be a shame to return home early because you didn't have the right work permit or enough money.

Timing

The sooner you start preparing for an overseas trip, the better. Bureaucracy in some of the world's poorer countries can be extremely slow or unpredictable. At the very least it's useful to have room and time to manoeuvre if something goes wrong.

As a general rule of thumb, if you are planning to go abroad for more than a year it's a good idea to start planning at least a year before you hope to go. If you are going for less than a year you should start your preparations between six and twelve months before your departure date.

Checklists

In either case, start by making lists of things to do and matters to be dealt with before you go. In the early stages it can be quite a rough list, but you'll refine it as you go along. Here are a few things that are probably worth putting on your list:

♦ *Passport* – is it up to date and if you are going overseas for two years do you have at least two more years to run on it?

♦ *Visas, work permits and criminal records* – does the country you are going to require these and how far in advance do you need to sort them out? Will the organisation you are going with arrange visas for you?

♦ *Inoculations* – you need to sort yourself out on these as soon as possible. Some can't be given within a certain time of others being given. Some countries might require proof that you have been vaccinated against particular diseases. You can find out which inoculations you need from your own GP, from British Airways Travel Clinics or from MASTA (Medical Advisory Service for Travellers).

◆ *Medication* – if you regularly take any medications (whether contraceptives or drugs for controlling a condition) you'll need to check if they are available where you are going. If not you'll need to check if they can be stored safely or if someone is willing to send them to you at regular intervals.

◆ *Insurance* – does the organisation you are going with provide this and if so what does it cover? If it isn't provided you'll need to get some. Also, what about insuring any property you are leaving behind?

◆ *Accommodation* – there and here. Sending agencies usually provide accommodation, but do you know what to expect? Will it have an inside toilet or an outside pit latrine? Will it have pots, pans and curtains? Will you need adapters for your electrical plugs? Also, what will you do with your home in the UK while you are gone? If you rent it out, what if your tenant leaves after a month – will you have enough money to continue paying the mortgage? If you are a tenant yourself will you have somewhere to stay if you have to return suddenly?

◆ *Clothing* – what will you need to take (what will the weather be like)? What will you be able to get overseas?

◆ *Luggage* – what's the weight restriction (both in terms of what you are prepared to carry and what airline companies will allow you)? Knowing how much you can take will help you to prioritise what to take.

- *Diet* – do you have any special needs and if so will you be able to meet them in the country you are going to?

- *Money* – even if you are getting paid while abroad, will it be enough? You need to try to find out what a 'shopping basket' of things like bread, meat, vegetables, milk, beer, clothes, stamps and paper costs in the country you are going to. How much money will you take and how will you keep it safe? Talk to other people who have been to the same place (or at least have had a similar experience). Find out how much money they got through, and remember, it's almost always more costly than you think it will be. If you are going for a long time it might be a good idea to open a bank account there – what will you need in order to do this?

- *Transport* – how will you get around? If you are expected to drive what kind of driving licence will you need? Will you be insured for driving? Will it be worth buying a vehicle and what can you afford?

- *Communications* – how will you stay in touch with people back home? How remote is it where you are going?

- *Paperwork* – who needs to know you're going – friends, family, the bank, the doctor, the landlord, the council...?

- *Language* – what's the spoken language and will you need to learn it? Is there any way you can start learning now?

Some or all of these issues will apply to you, though the list is not exhaustive because each person has different circumstances to accommodate.

When you have your list it should be pretty obvious which ones need dealing with first. Things like visas, health matters and your finances should be at the top of your list because not dealing with them could well mean not going.

Raising the money

If you are going overseas with an organisation that asks you to contribute towards costs, you may need to raise some money (amounts can vary from a few pounds to several thousands). Raising money is hard work, but you will gather useful skills and contacts along the way and you could have a lot of fun. You'll probably raise most of the money through sponsorship and there are several sources for this:

♦ friends and family – and friends and family of friends and family
♦ neighbours
♦ your local church
♦ local businesses
♦ national businesses with offices or stores in your area
♦ local Rotary, Round Table and Lions clubs
♦ clubs that you are a member of.

It's also worth contacting your local newspaper if you are organising a sponsored event because they might give you some publicity and that will help you get more money.

Being culturally prepared

It's important that you do some cultural preparation, at the very least to minimise the risk of offending someone. If you have to live and work in a community the more you understand about the way it works the easier your time will be and the more enjoyable too.

But bear in mind that adapting to a new culture can be very challenging and you will have to adjust your ideas as you go along. We all carry our own 'cultural baggage', which is virtually impossible to shake off. There are two general rules of thumb for living in another culture:

1. don't make assumptions
2. don't challenge.

It's all too easy to make the wrong assumptions and a good example of this is thinking that it's OK for men to wear shorts in a Muslim country because it's only women that aren't allowed to show their legs. But villagers in Uzbekistan have thrown stones at European men because they wore shorts. Instead of making assumptions, observe what people do and ask questions. Don't be afraid to ask – it shows that you have respect and that you are interested.

It can be difficult not to criticise the ways of a society that is very different from yours. They may appear unfair, perhaps even cruel – but avoid the temptation to challenge. In some countries, for example, women are legally the property of men and cannot have their own bank accounts or make any decisions affecting the family. Of course, you can always draw comparisons with the situation back home, but you should never openly declare that what exists in another culture is wrong (or worse, use loaded language like 'cruel' or 'barbaric'). No matter how much you disagree with something, you cannot go in guns blazing or you are likely to give offence and could even be sent home.

You can get a lot of information about the culture of the country you are going to from films, books, embassies and hopefully from the organisation you are going with. If possible, talk to as many people as you can who have been to or lived in the country in question. You will hear lots of contradictions and that will reinforce the need not to make assumptions, but there will also be lots of very useful information.

FINDING WORK BEFORE YOU GO OR WHEN YOU ARRIVE

If you decide to go overseas with an organisation that recruits (volunteers or paid staff) in the UK your preparation should be made a lot easier because the organisation should be able to provide help and advice on many issues – especially work permits, health matters and so on.

However, some people decide to go overseas to do voluntary work and they enhance the sense of adventure by arranging as little in advance as possible. It can be done, but it isn't easy. You should still make sure you are clear about the need for work permits and get as much information as you can from the country's embassy in the UK. If they can provide you with addresses of voluntary organisations in their country you will at least have a starting point.

Otherwise, when you arrive you will have to start networking very fast – asking people you meet if there is any local project going on, contacting churches, newspapers, colleges and any other institution that might know of someone that knows someone who runs a project.

You'll also need to make sure you have a solid financial base to work from.

RETURNING HOME

Another thing to consider if you want to go overseas is how you will adjust to life back in the UK afterwards. Many people experience greater 'culture shock' returning home than going away, especially if they have been on a long-term project. Check to see what kind of support the organisation you intend to go with offers to returning volunteers.

CASE STUDIES

Dennis Webster, science teacher

'I went to Botswana in 1989. I'd been living with my partner, Alison, for a few years and we decided that she would come with me. The thing was she could only stay on a three-month residence permit if she didn't have a job or if we weren't married! We were told the chances of her getting a job were slim, so after a lot of thought we decided to get married. Looking back I suppose I never thought going overseas would affect my life in that way.

'Anyway, I kept renewing my contract and we ended up staying in Botswana for eight years, during which time we had two children. Alison never did find a job so the finances were very tight. Having said that, we had a wonderful time and the worst thing about it was coming back to the UK. Everything is so rushed here and no one has time for anyone else. We've been back almost a year now and while the kids have adjusted I don't think we have yet.'

Jay Hall, student

'Apart from making sure I had the right inoculations and the right paperwork, there wasn't much else I got right when I went abroad. The reality only started to sink in when I got off the plane in the sweltering heat and saw this little airport building at the side of the runway. I didn't know a thing about the country apart from what I'd read in wildlife magazines.

'I managed to find a cheap hotel room and then I just froze. I didn't know who to contact, where to start. Added to that there was no light bulb in my room and no kettle to boil water with. I did eventually manage to find a local conservation group, but I was totally unprepared for their first question – 'what can you do?' I just thought they'd be grateful for my help if I just turned up. Naïve to say the least.

'I realised pretty quickly I was getting nowhere and decided to cut my trip short and save some money. I'll go again, but I'll be much better prepared and I'll have some skills to offer.'

Rupinder Kaur, field officer, South Africa

'Competition for paid jobs overseas can be very intense. I was working for an overseas charity and I'd been on working trips abroad that totalled about six months over four years. But I wanted to be a field officer – basically managing the organisation's operations in a particular country – and I didn't have any voluntary experience overseas, which is really crucial. So I applied to another overseas organisation to be a volunteer. There were no guarantees I'd be acceptable, just because I worked in the sector, but I did make it and then ended up spending three years in Papua New Guinea (or PNG as everybody calls it). The job I was sent to do was obviously my priority, but I helped out at the Field Office whenever I could. I started applying for field officer jobs even before I left PNG and eventually was offered this post, which is based in Johannesburg.'

CHECKLIST

♦ How long before going should you start planning?
♦ What factors should you consider in your practical pre-parations?
♦ What rules of thumb are useful in adapting to different cultures?

USEFUL RESOURCES

Useful addresses

British Airways Travel Clinics. Tel: 0845 779 9977 to find your nearest one. There are more than 30 in the UK.

MASTA (Medical Advisory Service for Travellers), London School of Hygiene and Tropical Medicine, Keppel Street, London WC1 7HT. Tel: (020) 7631 4408. www.masta.org E-mail: enquiries@masta.uk MASTA have information about immunisations and medical conditions overseas.

World Service Enquiry, Room 233 Bon Marché Centre, 241–251 Ferndale Road, London SW9 8BJ. Tel: (020) 7770 3274. www.wse.org.uk E-mail:wse@cabroad.org.uk A general enquiry and guidance service for people wanting to work overseas long-term, short-term, paid and voluntary.

Your local reference library should be able to help you find the addresses of embassies and consulates.

Sending agencies

British Red Cross, 44 Moorfields, London EC2Y 9AL. Tel: 0870 170 7000. www.redcross.org.uk E-mail: information@redcross.org.uk

ICD/CIIR (International Cooperation for Development), Unit 3, Canonbury Yard, 190A New North Road, London N1 7BJ. Tel: (020) 7354 0883. www.ciir.org E-mail: ciir@ciir.org A development organisation working in Africa and South America.

International Health Exchange (IHE), 1 Great George Streeet, London SW1P 3AA. Tel: (020) 7233 1100. www.ihe.org.uk E-mail: info@ihe.org.uk IHE keep a register of health workers who want to work in emergency or development posts. They also publish a development and jobs magazine called *The Health Exchange*.

International Service, Hunter House, 57 Goodramgate, York YO1 2LS. Tel: (01904) 647799. www.is@internationalservice.org.uk E-mail: unais_uk@geo2.poptel.org.uk A development organisation working in West Africa, Latin America and the Middle East.

MERLIN (Medical Emergency Relief International), 4th Floor, 56–64 Leonard Street, London EC2A 4LT. Tel: (020) 7065 0800. www.merlin.org.uk Provides emergency medical relief in disaster areas around the world.

Oxfam, 274 Banbury Road, Oxford OX2 7DZ. Tel: 0870 3332700. www.oxfam.org.uk E-mail: oxfam@oxfam.org.uk

RedR – Register of Engineers for Disaster Relief, 1 Great

George Street, London SW1P 3AA. Tel: (020) 7233
3116. www. redr.org E-mail: info@redr.org

Skillshare International, 126 New Walk, Leicester LE1
7JA. Tel: (0116) 254 1862. www. skillshare.org
E-mail: info@skillshare.org A development organisation working in Africa and Asia.

VSO, 317 Putney Bridge Road, London SW15 2PN. Tel:
(020) 8780 7200. www.vso.org.uk
E-mail: infoservices@vso.org.uk A development organisation working around the world.

Further reading

Bugs, Bites and Bowels, Dr Jane Wilson-Howarth (Cado-
gan Books, 2002).

The International Directory of Voluntary Work (Vacation
Work, 2002).

The *Rough Guide...* series is worth looking at for the
country you are going to.

Planning Your Gap Year, Nick Vandome (How To Books,
2005).

Worldwide Volunteering, compiled by Roger Potter (How
To Books, 2004). This book complements the Worldwide Volunteering for Young People search and match
database.

9

Working with People

USING THIS CHAPTER

The organisations listed here focus their work mainly on people. The nature of that work can vary enormously, from advising to campaigning, from training to giving medical treatment.

The names of many organisations explain quite well what they do – if it doesn't there is a short explanation after the address.

The organisations are divided into categories so that you can find what you are looking for more easily. Some organisations may fit into one or more categories. In this case they have been put into the most obvious one.

This is obviously a very small selection of the hundreds of thousands of voluntary sector organisations that exist in the country. If the one you are looking for is not listed here, it does not mean it doesn't exist. Try contacting an organisation in a related category – they may have contact details for other groups and organisations. For example, if you are looking for an organisation that deals with the issue of glue sniffing, contact one of the organisations in the addiction category to see if they can put you in touch with the right people.

Organisations have been selected to try to meet as wide a range of interests as possible. The political parties (Conservative, Green, Labour and Liberal) have been included because although not strictly voluntary organisations they are a focus of voluntary activity for many people.

DIRECTORY OF RELEVANT ORGANISATIONS

Addiction

Addaction, 67–69 Cowcross Street, London EC1M 6BP. Tel: (020) 7251 5860. www.addaction.org.uk. E-mail: info@addaction.org.uk Drug and alcohol addiction work.

Addiction Recovery Agency, 61 Queen Charlotte Street, Bristol BS1 4HQ. Tel: (0117) 930 0282.
www.addictionrecover.org.uk
E-mail: info@:addictionrecovery.org.uk Treatment and rehabilitation for addicts committed to abstinence.

ADFAM National (The National Charity for Families of Drug Users), 32–36 Loman Street, London SE1 0EH. Tel: (020) 7928 8898. www.adfam.org.uk
E-mail: admin@adfam.org.uk

ASH – Action on Smoking and Health, 102 Clifton Street, London EC2A 4HW. Tel: (020) 7739 5902. www.ash.org.uk E-mail: enquiries@ash.org.uk

Chemical Dependency Centre Ltd, 11 Redcliffe Gardens, London SW10 9BG. Tel: (020) 7351 0217.
www.thecdc.org.uk E-mail: info:@thecdc.org.uk

GamCare, Units 2 & 3, Baden Place, London SE1 1YW. Tel: (020) 7378 5200.
www.gamcare.org.uk E-mail: info@gamcare.org.uk
Working with gambling addiction.

Hope UK, 25f Copperfield Street, London SE1 0EN. Tel:

(020) 7928 0848. www.hopeuk.org Encourages children and young people away from drugs and drink.

Life Education Centres, County House, 14 Hatton Gardens, London EC1N 8AT. Tel: 0870 770 2455. www.lifeducation.org.uk Educating young people about drug abuse and AIDS.

Re-Solv – The Society for the Prevention of Solvent and Volatile Substance Abuse, 30a High Street, Stone, Staffordshire ST15 8AW. Tel: (01785) 817855. www.re-solv.org E-mail: information@re-solv.org

Advice, counselling and rights

Advice UK, New London Bridge House, 25 London Bridge Street, London SE1 9ST. Tel: (020) 7407 4070. www.adviceuk.org.uk E-mail: general@adviceuk.org.uk Promoting independent advice services.

Befrienders International, now run by Samaritans (see below). www.befrienders.org Supporting the suicidal and others in distress.

Befriending Network, Claremont, 24 White Lion Street, London N1 9PD. Tel: (020) 7689 2448. www.befriending.net E-mail: info@befriending.net Helping the critically ill and their carers.

Brook, 421 Highgate Studios, 53–79 Highgate Road, London, NW5 1TL. Tel: (020) 7284 6040. www.brook.org.uk E-mail: admin@brookcentres.org.uk Sex and contraception education.

Childline, 45 Folgate Street, London E1 6GL. Tel: (020) 7650 3200. www.childline.org.uk E-mail: info:childline.org.uk

National Association of Citizens' Advice Bureaux (NA-CAB), 115–123 Pentonville Road, London N1 9LZ.

Tel: (020) 7833 2181. www.citizensadvice.org.uk

Relate: National Marriage Guidance, Herbert Gray College, Little Church Street, Rugby, Warwickshire CV21 3AP. Tel: (01788) 573241. www.relate.org.uk

Samaritans (The Samaritans), The Upper Mill, Kingston Road, Ewell, Surrey KT17 2AF. Tel: (020) 8394 8300. www.samaritans.org.uk

E-mail: admin@samaritans.org.uk

Westminster Pastoral Foundation, 23 Kensington Square, London W8 5HN. Tel: (020) 7937 6956. www.wpf.org.uk National counselling and psychotherapy service.

Youth Access, 1 Taylors Yard, 67 Alderbrook Road, London SW12 8AD. Tel: (020) 8772 9900. www.youthaccess.org.uk

E-mail: admin@youthaccess.org.uk Encouraging the growth of young people's counselling and advisory services.

Arts and culture

AFS – International Youth Development, Leeming House, Vicar Lane, Leeds LS2 7JF. Tel: (0113) 242 6136. www.afsuk.org International exchange programmes.

British Association of Friends of Museums, Fonthill Cottages, Lewannick, Launceston, Cornwall PL15 7QE. www.bafm.org.uk

British Federation of Festivals, Festivals House, 198 Park Lane, Macclesfield, Cheshire SK11 6UD. Tel: 0870 7744 290/291. www.festivals.demon.co.uk

Dreams Come True Charity, York House, Knockhundred Row, Midhurst, West Sussex GU29 9DQ. Tel: (01730)

815 000 www.dctc.org.uk Email: info@dctc.org.uk

Dream Makers, 37 Marlborough Road, Castle Bromwich, Birmingham B36 0EH. Tel: (0121) 776 7144. Relief for children and families threatened by illness.

Live Music Now!, 4 Lower Belgrave Street, London, SW1W 0JL. www.livemusicnow.org

Music Education Council, 54 Elm Road, Hale, Altrincham, Cheshire WA15 9QP. Tel: (0161) 928 3085. www.mec.org.uk

National Campaign for the Arts, Pegasus House, 37–43 Sackville Street, London W1S 3EH. Tel: (020) 7333 0375. www.artscampaign.org.uk
Email: nca@artscampaign.org.uk

Public Art Development Trust, 80–82 Whitechapel High Street, London E1 7QX. Tel: (020) 7377 9070. www.padt.org.uk Commissions and produces public arts projects.

Business

Business in the Community, 137 Shepherdess Walk, London N1 7RQ. Tel: 0870 600 2482. www.bitc.org.uk
E-mail: information@bitc.org.uk

Prince's Trust, 18 Park Square East, London NW1 4LH. Tel: (020) 7543 1234. www.princes-trust.org.uk
E-mail: info@princes-trust.org.uk

Young Enterprise, Peterley House, Peterley Road, Oxford OX4 2TZ. Tel: (01865) 776845. www.young-enterprise.org.uk E-mail: info@young-enterprise.org.uk

Children

Action for Sick Children, 8 Wakley Street, London EC1V 7QE. Tel: (020) 7843 6444.

www.actionforsickchildren.org.uk

Anti-Bullying Campaign, 185 Tower Bridge Road, London SE1 2UF. Tel: (020) 7378 1446. Awareness and training programmes on bullying; also a telephone helpline.

Barnardo's, Tanners Lane, Barkingside, Ilford, Essex IG6 1QG. Tel: (020) 8550 8822. www.barnados.org.uk

Children's Society, Edward Rudolf House, Margery Street, London WC1X 0JL. Tel: (020) 7841 4400. www.childrenssociety.org.uk

E-mail: info@childrenssociety.org.uk

Farms for City Children, Nethercott House, Iddesleigh, Winkleigh, Devon EX19 8BG. Tel: (01837) 810573. www.farmsforcitychildren.co.uk

Grandparents' Association, Moot House, The Stow, Harlow, Essex CM20 3AG. Tel: (01279) 428040. www.grandparents-association.org.uk

National Society for the Prevention of Cruelty to Children (NSPCC), Weston House, 42 Curtain Road, London EC2A 3NH. Tel: (020) 7825 2500. www.nspcc.org.uk E-mail: info@nspcc.org.uk

NCH (National Children's Homes), 85 Highbury Park, London N5 1UD. Tel: (020) 774 7000. www.nch.org.uk Child care charity.

Rainer, Rectory Lodge, High Street, Brasted, Westerham, Kent TN16 1JF. Tel: (01959) 578200. www.raineronline.org Helping children at risk.

Save the Children UK, 1 St John's Lane, London EC1M 4AR. Tel: (020) 7012 6400. www.savethechildren.org.uk

SOS Children's Villages UK, 59 St Andrews Street, Cambridge CB2 3BZ. Tel: (01223) 365589.

www.soschildrensvillages.org.uk Caring for homeless, orphaned and abandoned children.

Community

Community Matters (National Federation of Community Organisations), 12–20 Baron Street, London N1 9LL. Tel: (020) 7837 7887. www.communitymatters.org.uk

Community Transport Association, Highbank, Halton Street, Hyde, Cheshire SK14 2NY. Tel: (01613) 511475. www.communitytransport.com

Inter-Action Trust, HMS President (1918), King's Reach, Victoria Embankment, London EC4Y 0HJ. Tel: (020) 7583 2652. Using entrepreneurial skills for community benefit.

National Coalition-Building Institute (NCBI), The Learning Exchange, Wygston's House, Applegate, Leicester LE1 5LD. www.ncbiuk.org.uk
E-mail: info@ncbileic.org.uk Working to eliminate prejudice and discrimination.

Disability

British Council of Disabled People, Litchurch Plaza, Litchurch Lane, Derby DE24 8AA. Tel: (01332) 295 551. www.bcodp.org.uk

Disability Sport England, Unit 4G, N17 Studios, 784–788 High Road, Tottenham, London N17 0DA. Tel: (020) 8801 4466. www.disabilitysport.org.uk

Gardening for Disabled Trust, Frittenden House, Frittenden, Cranbrook, Kent TN17 2DG. Tel: (01580) 852120.

Leonard Cheshire, 30 Millbank, London SW1P 4QD. Tel: (020) 7802 8200. www.leonard-cheshire.org

Riding for the Disabled Association (RDA), Lavinia

Norfolk House, National Agricultural Centre, Stoneleigh Park, Kenilworth, Warwickshire CV8 2LY. Tel: (02476) 696510. www.riding-for-disabled.org.uk
Royal National Institute for the Blind (RNIB), 105 Judd Street, London WC1H 9NE. Tel: (020) 7388 1266. www.rnib.org.uk E-mail: rnib@rnib.org.uk
Ryder-Cheshire Volunteers, 13b Holly Court, Holly Farm Business Park, Honiley, Kenilworth, Warwickshire CV8 1NP. Tel: (01926) 485 446. www.rydercheshire.org.uk E-mail: info@rydercheshire.org.uk. Giving disabled people the opportunity to pursue activities in partnership with volunteers.
SCOPE, PO Box 833, Milton Keynes MK12 5NY. Tel: 0808 800 3333. www.scope.org.uk For people with cerebral palsy.
SENSE: The National Deaf-Blind and Rubella Association, 11–13 Clifton Terrace, Finsbury Park, London N4 3SR. Tel: (020) 7272 7774. www.sense.org.uk E-mail: enquiries@sense.org.uk
Vitalise, 12 City Forum, 250 City Road, London EC1V 8AF. Tel: 0845 345 1972. www.vitalise.org.uk Providing holidays for disabled adults, children and their carers.

Ethnicity and race
Anne Frank Trust UK, Star House, 104–108 Grafton Road, London NW5 4BD. Tel: (020) 7284 5858. www.annefrank.org.uk E-mail: afet@efet.org.uk Education for mutual respect, compassion and social justice.
Bangladeshis for Equal Rights, Suite F, Radclyffe House, 66–68 Hagley Road, Birmingham B16 8PF. Tel: (0121) 454 5220.

Chinese Information and Advice Centre, 104–108 New Oxford Street, London W10 1LP. Tel: (020) 7323 1538.

Commission for Racial Equality, St Dunstan's House, 201–11 Borough High Street, London SE1 1GZ. www.cre.gov.uk. E-mail: info@cre.gov.uk

Confederation of Indian Organisations (UK), 5 Westminster Bridge Road, London SE1 7XW. Tel: (020) 7928 9889. www.cio.org.uk E-mail: headoffice@cio.org.uk

Minority Rights Group, 54 Commercial Street, London E1 6LT. Tel: (020) 7422 4200. www.minorityrights.org E-mail: minority.rights@mrgmail.org

Union of Muslim Organisations of UK and Eire (UMO), 109 Campden Hill Road, London W8 7TL. Tel: (020) 7229 0538.

Health

Action Against Allergy, PO Box 278, Twickenham TW1 4QQ. Tel: (020) 8892 4949.
www.actionagainstallergy.co.uk

Asthma UK, Providence House, Providence Place, London N1 0NT. Tel: (020) 7226 2260. www.asthma.org.uk

Bristol Cancer Help Centre, Grove House, Cornwallis Grove, Clifton, Bristol BS8 4PG. Tel: (0117) 980 9500. www.bristolcancerhelp.org
E-mail: info@bristolcancerhelp.org

British Red Cross, Moorfields House, Moorfields, London EC2Y 9AL. Tel: (020) 7235 5454. www.redcross.org.uk E-mail: information@redcross.org.uk

Eating Disorders Association (EDA), Wensum House, 103 Prince of Wales Road, Norwich, Norfolk N1 1DW. Tel: 0870 770 3257. www.edauk.com
E-mail: info@edauk.com

Mangreen Trust, Mangreen Hall, Swardeston, Norfolk NR14 8DD. Tel: (01508) 570 444.
www.mangreen.co.uk Provision of complementary and alternative medicine and therapies.

Mind (National Association for Mental Health), Granta House, 15–19 Broadway, London E15 4BQ. Tel: (020) 8519 2122. www.mind.org.uk
E-mail: contact@mind.org.uk

National Phobics Society, Zion CRC, 339 Stretford Road, Hulme, Manchester M15 4ZY. Tel: 0870 7700 456. www.phobics-society.org.uk

No Panic, 93 Branch Farm Way, Randlay, Telford, Shropshire TF3 2JQ. Tel: (01952) 590 005.
www.no-panic.org.uk Helping people with anxiety disorders.

Overeaters Anonymous, PO Box 19, Stretford, Manchester M32 9EB. Tel: (07000) 784 985. www.oa.org

St John Ambulance, 27 St John's Lane, London EC1M 4BU. Tel: (020) 324 4000. www.sja.org.uk

Terrence Higgins Trust (THT), 52–54 Gray's Inn Road, London WC1X 8JU. Tel: (020) 7831 0330.
www.tht.org.uk E-mail: info@tht.org.uk Support and education on AIDS and HIV.

Homes and homelessness

Crisis, 64 Commercial Street, London E1 6LT. Tel: 0870 011 3335. www.crisis.org.uk
E-mail: www.enquries@crisis.org.uk Helping single homeless people.

Homeless International, Queens House, 16 Queens Road, Coventry, West Midlands CV1 3DF. Tel: (0247) 663 2802. www.homeless-international.org

E-mail: admin@homeless-international.org

Rural Housing Trust, 8 Graphite Square, Vauxhall, London SE11 5EE. Tel: (020) 7793 3304.
www.ruralhousing.org.uk
E-mail: info@:ruralhousing.org.uk

Shelter, 88 Old Street, London EC1V 9HU. Tel: (020) 7505 2000. www.shelter.org.uk
E-mail: info@shelter.org.uk

Simon Community, PO Box 1187, London NW5 4HW. Tel: (020) 7485 6639. www.simoncommunity.org.uk
Providing relief and care for people sleeping rough.

Leisure

Backpackers Club, 11 Moreton Avenue, Claycross, Chesterfield, Derbyshire S45 9PX. Tel: 01246 251509.

British Cycling Federation (BCF), National Cycling Centre, Stuart Street, Manchester M11 4DQ. Tel: 0870 871 2000. www.bcf.uk.com

DoBE.org, 6 Blackstock Mews, Blackstock Road, London N4 2BT. Tel: (020) 7359 8391. www.dobe.org Usuing the Internet to increase participatory activities in major cities.

English Civil War Society, 70 Hailgate, Howden, Humberside DN14 7ST. Tel: (01430) 430695.
www.english-civil-war-society.org

Family Holiday Association, 16 Mortimer Street, London W1T 3JL. Tel: (020) 7436 3304. www.fhaonline.org.uk
E-mail:info@fhaonline.org.uk

National Caving Association (NCA), Monomark House, 27 Old Gloucester Street, London WC1N 3XX. Tel: (0114) 230 3575 (evenings and weekends only).
www.nca.org.uk E-mail: admin@nca.org.uk

Youth Hostels Association (YHA), PO Box 6030, Dimple Road, Matlock, Derbyshire DE4 3XA. Tel: (01629) 592641. www.yha.org.uk

Offenders and victims

Aftermath, PO Box 414, Sheffield S4 7RT. Tel: (0114) 275 3883. www.aftermathuk.org.uk Supporting the families of serious offenders.

Apex Trust, St Alphage House, Wingate Annexe, 2 Fore Street, London EC2Y 5DA. Tel: (020) 7638 5931. www.apextrust.com Helping ex-offenders to improve their chances of finding paid work.

Campaign Against Drinking and Driving, 14 Fontwell Court, Bristol BS14 3BA. Tel: (01275) 892 225. www.cadd.org.uk

Howard League for Penal Reform, 1 Ardleigh Road, London N1 4HS. Tel: (020) 7249 7373. www.howardleague.org
E-mail: info@howardleague.org

Independent Care after Incest and Rape, Gatehouse, Whiteways, Great Chesterford, Essex CB10 1NX. Tel: (01799) 530 520. www.icair.org.uk

Independent Custody Visiting Association, 16–18 Whidborne Street, London WC1H 8EZ. Tel: (020) 7837 0078. www.icva.org.uk

Mediation UK, Alexander House, Telephone Avenue, Bristol BS1 4BS. Tel: (0117) 904 6661. www.meditationuk.org.uk
E-mail: enquiry@mediationuk.org.uk

NACRO (National Association for the Care and Resettlement of Offenders), 169 Clapham Road, London SW9 0PU. Tel: (020) 7582 6500. www.nacro.org.uk

National Organisation for the Treatment of Abusers, PO
Box 356, Hull HU12 8WR. www.nota.org.uk

Prison Advice and Care Trust, Lincoln House, 1–3 Brixton Road, London SW9 6DE. Tel: (020) 7582 1313.
www.imprisonment.org.uk

SOVA, 1st Floor, Chichester House, 37 Brixton Road,
London W9 6DZ. Tel: (020) 7793 0404.
E-mail: mail@sova.org.uk Promoting community in-
volvement in caring for and resettling offenders.

Victim Support, www.victimsupport.org See the website
for details of activities and contacts in Scotland, Northern Ireland, England and Wales, and the Republic of
Ireland.

Victims of Crime Trust, 2 York Street, Twickenham,
Middlesex TW1 3LE. Tel: (020) 8744 0999.
www.crimevictims.org.uk
E-mail: info@crimevictims.org.uk

Old age

Age Concern England, Astral House, 1268 London Road,
London SW16 4ER. Tel: (020) 8765 7200.
www.ace.org.uk E-mail: ace@ace.org.uk

Age-Link, 9 Narborough Close, Ickenham, Middlesex
UB10 8TN. Tel: (01895) 676689. www.age-link.org.uk

Aid for the Aged in Distress, 54 London Road, Morden,
Surrey SM4 5BE. www.agedistress.org.uk

Help The Aged, 207–221 Pentonville Road, London N1
9UZ. Tel: (020) 7278 1114. www.helptheaged.org.uk
E-mail: info@helptheaged.org.uk

Third Age Trust (U3A), 19 East Street, Bromley, Kent
BR1 1QH. Tel: (020) 8466 6139. www.u3a.org.uk

Peace, poverty and development

Campaign for Nuclear Disarmament (CND), 162 Holloway Road, London N7 8DQ. Tel: (020) 7700 2393. www.cnd.uk.org E-mail: enquiries@cnduk.org

Child Poverty Action Group (CPAG), 94 White Lion Street, London N1 9PF. Tel: (020) 7837 7979. www.cpag.org.uk E-mail: staff@cpag.org.uk

Development Education Association (DEA), 33 Corsham Street, London N1 6DR. Tel: (020) 7490 8108. www.dea.org.uk E-mail: dea@dea.org.uk

Fairtrade Foundation, Room 204, 16 Baldwin Gardens, Hatton Square, London EC1N 7RJ. Tel: (020) 7405 5942. www.fairtrade.org.uk

Family Welfare Association (FWA), 501–505 Kingsland Road, London E8 4AU. Tel: (020) 7245 6251.

Mines Clearance International (MCI), PO Box 4100, Worthing, West Sussex BN11 3WP. Tel: (01302) 366388. www.landmineclearance.org.uk

One World Action (OWA), Bradley's Close, White Lion Street, London N1 9PF. Tel: (020) 7833 4075. www.oneworldaction.org
E-mail: owa@oneworldaction.org

Peace Pledge Union (PPU), 1 Peace Passage, London N7 0BT. Tel: (020) 7424 9444. www.ppu.org.uk
E-mail: enquiry@ppu.org.uk

Saferworld, The Grayston Centre, 28 Charles Square, London N1 6HT. Tel: (020) 7324 4646. www.saferworld.org.uk
E-mail: general@saferworld.org.uk

Politics and campaigning

Action for Southern Africa, (ACTSA), 28 Penton Street,

London N1 9SA. Tel: (020) 7833 3133. www.actsa.org

Amnesty International UK, 99–119 Rosebery Avenue, London EC1R 4RE. Tel: (020) 7814 6200. www.amnesty.org.uk Email: info@amnesty.org.uk

Anti-Slavery International, Thomas Clarkson House, The Stableyard, Broomgrove Road, London SW9 9TL. Tel: (020) 7501 8920. www.antislavery.org E-mail: info@antislavery.org

Campaign Against Arms Trade (CAAT), 11 Goodwin Street, London N4 3HQ. Tel: (020) 7281 0297. www.caat.org.uk E-mail: enquiries@caat.org.uk

Charter 88, 6 Cynthia Street, London N1 9JF. Tel: (020) 8880 6088. www.charter88.org.uk Campaigning for a written constitution for the UK.

Conservative Party, Central Office, 32 Smith Square, London SW1P 3HH. Tel: (020) 7222 9000. www.conservatives.com

Green Party, 1a Waterloo Road, London N19 5NJ. Tel: (020) 7272 4474. www.greenparty.org.uk E-mail: office@greenparty.org.uk

Labour Party, 16 Old Queen Street, London SW1H 9HP. Tel: 08705 900200. www.labour.org.uk

Liberal Democrats, 4 Cowley Street, London SW1P 3NB. Tel: (020) 7222 7999. www.libdems.org.uk

New Politics Network, 6 Cynthia Street, London N1 9JF. Tel: (020) 7278 4443. www.new-politics.org

Sex and sexuality

Gender Identity Consultancy Services (GICS), BM Box 5434, London WC1N 3XX. Tel: (020) 7828 9575. E-mail: gics@aol.com Support for transsexuals and their families.

London Lesbian and Gay Switchboard, PO Box 7324, London N1 9QS. Tel: (020) 7837 7324. www.llgs.org.uk E-mail: admin@llgs.org.uk

Stonewall, 46 Grosvenor Gardens, London SW1W 0EB. Tel: (020) 7881 9440. www.stonewall.org.uk E-mail: info@stonewall.org.uk Campaigning for equal rights for lesbians and gay men.

Women

ABANTU for Development, 1 Winchester House, 11 Cranmer Road, London SW9 6EJ. www.abantu.org Women's development programmes in Africa.

British Housewives' League (BHL), Birchfield House, Mounton Road, Chepstow NP16 5BS Tel: (020) 8445 4848. www.housewives.freeuk.com

CHANGE, Unit 19–20 Unity Business Centre, 26 Round-hay Road, Leeds LS7 1AB. Tel: (0113) 243 0202. E-mail: changepeople@btconnect.com Education, consultancy and research on women's issues.

Feminist Audio Books (FAB), PO Box 83, Ruislip, Middlesex, HA4 9UL. Tel: (020) 8582 2899.

National Alliance of Women's Organisations (NAWO), PO Box 25766, London SW19 4WR. Tel: (020) 7266 5056.

WinVisible: Women with Visible and Invisible Disabilities, Crossroads Women's Centre, 230A Kentish Town Road, London NW5 2AB. Tel: (020) 7482 2496.

Womankind Worldwide, 32–37 Cowper Street, London EC2A 4AW. Tel: (020) 7549 5700. www.womankind.org.uk E-mail: info@womankind.org.uk

Women Against Rape (WAR), PO Box 287, London NW6

5QU. Tel: (020) 7482 2496. www.womenagainstrape.-
net

Women Welcome Women Worldwide, 88 Easton Street,
High Wycombe, Buckinghamshire HP11 1LT. Tel:
(01494) 465441. www.womenwelcomewomen.org.uk

Women's Environmental Network (WEN), PO Box
30626, London E1 1TZ. Tel (020) 7481 9004.
www.wen.org.uk

Women's Health, 52 Featherstone Street, London EC1Y
8RT. Tel: (020) 7251 6333.
www.womenshealthlondon.org.uk

Women's Sports Foundation, Victoria House, Bloomsbury Square, London WC1B 4SE. www.wsf.org.uk
E-mail: info@wsf.org.uk

Youth

Forest School Camps, 75 Thomas's Road, London N4
2QJ. www.fsc.org.uk

Girlguiding UK (Guide Association), 17–19 Buckingham
Palace Road, London SW1W 0PT. Tel: (020) 7834 6242.
www.guides.org.uk Email: chq@girlguiding.org.uk

Ocean Youth Trust, Tel: (02392) 528421. www.oyc.org.uk
A cooperative of six charities around the UK.

Scout Association, Gilwell Park, Bury Road, Chingford,
London E4 7QW. Tel: (020) 8433 7100.
www.scouts.org.uk E-mail: info.centre@scouts.org.uk

Students Partnership Worldwide, 17 Dean's Yard, London SW1P 3PB. Tel: (020) 7222 0138. www.spw.org
Opportunties to live and work in partnership with local
volunteers in Africa and Asia on health or environment
projects.

UK Youth, Kirby House, 20–24 Kirby Street, London

EC1N 8TS. Tel: (020) 7242 4045. www.ukyouth.org

Voice for the Child in Care, Unit 4, Pride Court, 80–82 White Lion Street, London N1 9PF. Tel: (020) 7833 5792. www.vcc-uk.org E-mail: info@vcc-uk.org

YMCA, 640 Forest Road, London E17 3DZ. Tel: (020) 8520 5599. www.ymca.org.uk
E-mail: info@ymca.org.uk

YWCA, Clarendon House, 52 Cornmarket Street, Oxford OX1 3EJ. Tel: (01865) 304200. www.ywca-gb.org.uk
E-mail: info@ywca-gb.org.uk

(10)

Working for Animals and the Environment

USING THIS CHAPTER

Animal and environment organisations are very popular and there are lots of opportunities at voluntary and paid levels. However, competition for some positions (even voluntary ones) can be quite intense.

Organisations are listed alphabetically under the different groupings and are placed where they (hopefully) make most sense.

If you are interested in a particular animal, plant or environmental issue and it does not seem to be covered here, try contacting a related organisation to see if they can help. For example, if you are looking for an organisation that is concerned with organic gardening, it may be worth contacting the National Council for the Conservation of Plants and Gardens or one of the organisations listed under 'natural environment'. Either may be able to point you in the right direction.

As in Chapter 9, organisations have been chosen to try to represent as wide a range of interests as possible.

DIRECTORY OF RELEVANT ORGANISATIONS

Animals

The Bats Conservation Trust, Unit 2, 15 Cloisters House, 8 Battersea Park Road, London SW8 4BG. Tel: (020) 7627 2629. www.bats.org.uk
E-mail: enquiries@bats.org.uk

Blue Cross, Shilton Road, Burford, Oxfordshire OX18 4PF. Tel: (01993) 822657. www.bluecross.org.uk Veterinary and welfare care for domestic animals.

Born Free Foundation (BFF), 3 Grove House, Foundry Lane, Horsham, West Sussex RH13 5PL. Tel: (01403) 240170. www.bornfree.org.uk
E-mail: wildlife@bornfree.org.uk Investigating animal suffering in zoos and promoting preservation of wildlife habitats.

British Trust for Ornithology, BTO, The Nunnery, Thetford, Norfolk IP24 2PU. Tel: (01482) 750050. www.bto.org E-mail: info@bto.org

British Union for the Abolition of Vivisection (BUAV), 16a Crane Grove, London N7 8LB. Tel: (020) 7700 4888. www.buav.org E-mail: info@buav.org

Cats Protection, Natiuonal Cat Centre, Chelwood Gate, Haywards Heath, Sussex RH17 7TT. Tel: (08702) 099 099. www.cats.org.uk E-mail: info@cats.org.uk

Compassion in World Farming, 5a Charles Street, Petersfield, Hampshire GU32 3EH. Tel: (01730) 264208. www.ciwf.org.uk

The Donkey Sanctuary, Sidmouth, Devon EX10 0NU. Tel: (01395) 578 222. www.thedonkeysanctuary.org.uk

Greek Animal Welfare Fund, 1–2 Castle Lane, London SW1E 6DN. Tel: (020) 7828 9736. www.gawf.org.uk

Herpetological Conservation Trust (HCT), 655a Christch-

urch Road, Boscombe, Bournemouth BH1 4AP. Tel:
(01202) 391319. www.herpconstrust.org.uk

Humane Research Trust, Brook House, 29 Bramhall Lane
South, Bramhall, Cheshire SK7 2DN. Tel: (0161) 439
8041. www.humaneresearch.org.uk

International Fund for Animal Welfare, Camelford
House, 87–90 Albert Embankment, London SE1
9UD. Tel: (020) 7587 7600. www.ifaw.org

League Against Cruel Sports, Sparling House, 83–87 Union Street, London SE1 1SG. Tel: (020) 7403 6155.
www.league.uk.com

Mammal Society, 2B Inworth Street, London SW11 3EP.
Tel: (020) 7350 2200. www.mammal.org.uk

Rare Breeds Survival Trust, National Agricultural Centre, Stoneleigh Park, Kenilworth, Warwickshire CV8
2LG. Tel: (02476) 696551. www.rbst.org.uk

Royal Society for the Prevention of Cruelty to Animals
(RSPCA), Wilberforce Way, Southwater, Horsham,
West Sussex RH13 9RS. Tel: 0870 010 1181.
www.rspca.org.uk

Royal Society for the Protection of Birds (RSPB), The
Lodge, Sandy, Bedfordshire SG19 2DL. Tel: (01767)
680551. www.rspb.org.uk

National Search and Rescue Dog Association.
www.nsarda.org.uk

Sea Watch Foundation – The Cetacean Monitoring Unit,
11 Jersey Road, Oxford OX4 4RT. Tel: (01865) 764 794.
www.seawatchfoundation.org.uk

Whale and Dolphin Conservation Society (WDCS),
Brookfield House, 38 St Paul Street, Chippenham,
Wiltshire SN15 1LY. Tel: 0870 870 0027.
www.wdcs.org

World Society for the Protection of Animals (WSPA), 87–89 Albert Embankment, London SE1 7TP. Tel: (020) 7587 5000. www.wspa.org.uk
E-mail: wspa@wspa.org.uk
WWF UK, Panda House, Weyside Park, Godalming, Surrey GU7 1XR. Tel: (01483) 426444. www.wwf.org.uk

Plants

British Bryological Society (BBS), Ivy House, Wheelock Street, Middlewich, Cheshire CW10 9AB. www.britishbryologicalsociety.org.uk Promoting interest in study of mosses and liverworts.

International Tree Foundation, Sandy Lane, Crawley Down, Crawley, West Sussex RH10 4HS. Tel: 0870 774 4269. www.internationaltreefoundation.org.uk

National Council for the Conservation of Plants and Gardens (NCCPG), The Stable Courtyard, RHS Garden, Wisley, Woking, Surrey GU23 6QB. Tel: (01483) 211465. www.ncpg.com E-mail: info@ncpg.com

Natural environment

The Black Environment Network (BEN), 1st Floor, 60 High Street, Llanberis, Wales LL55 4EU. Tel: (01286) 870 715. www.ben-netowrk.org.uk
E-mail: uk-office@bennetwork.org.uk

Earthwatch Institute (Europe), 267 Banbury Road, Oxford OX2 7HT. Tel: (01865) 318 838. www.earthwatch.org/europe
E-mail: info@earthwatch.org.uk Conservation, education and research, including volunteer programmes.

The Rainforest Foundation UK, Suite A5, City Cloisters, 196 Old Street, London EC1V 9FR. Tel: (020) 6251

6345. www.rainforestfoundationuk.org

British Trust for Conservation Volunteers (BTCV), 80 York Way, London N1 9AG Tel: (020) 7843 4298. www.btcv.org E-mail: information@btcv.org.uk

Commonwork Land Trust (CLT), Bore Place, Chiddingstone, Edenbridge, Kent TN8 7AR. Tel: (01732) 463255. www.commonwork.org
E-mail: info@commonwork.org Education on environment.

Farming and Wildlife Advisory Group (FWAG), National Agricultural Centre, Stoneleigh Park, Kenilworth, Warwickshire CV8 2RX. Tel: (02476) 696699. www.fwag.org.uk E-mail: info@fwag.org.uk

Foundation for International Environment Law and Development (FIELD), 3 Endsleigh Street, London WC1H 0DD. Tel: (020) 7388 2117. www.field.org.uk
E-mail: field@field.org.uk

Friends of the Earth (FOE), 26–28 Underwood Street, London N1 7JQ. Tel: (020) 7490 1555. www.foe.co.uk
E-mail: info@foe.co.uk

Greenpeace, Canonbury Villas, London N1 2PN. Tel: (020) 7865 8100. www.greenpeace.org.uk
E-mail: info@uk.greenpeace.org

International Good Gardeners' Association (GGA), 4 Lisle Place, Wotton Under Edge, Gloucestershire GL12 7AZ. Tel: (01453) 520322.
www.goodgardners.org.uk

Marine Conservation Society (MCS), Unit 3, Wolf Business Park, Ross-on-Wye, Herefordshire HR9 5NB. Tel: (01989) 566017. www.mcsuk.org

WWOOF (Willing Workers on Organic Farms), PO Box 2675, Lewes, East Sussex BN7 1RB. Tel: (01273)

476286. www.wwoof.org.uk

Built environment

British Urban Regeneration Association (BURA), 63–66
Hatton Garden, Londn EC1N 8LE. Tel: (020) 7539
4030. www.bura.org.uk E-mail: info:@bura.org.uk

Noise Abatement Society, 44 Grande Parade, Brighton,
East Sussex BN2 9QA. Tel: (01273) 682 223.
www.noiseabatementsociety.com
E-mail: nas@noiseabatementsociety.fsnet.co.uk

Free Form Arts Trust, Hothouse, 274 Richmond Road,
London E8 3QW. Tel: (020) 7249 3394.
www. freeform.org.uk
E-mail: contact@freeform.org.uk Community environmental work.

Groundwork, 85–87 Cornwall Street, Birmingham B3
3BY. Tel: (0121) 236 8565. www.groundwork.org.uk
E-mail: info@groundwork.org.uk Working with local
businesses, local government and communities to improve environments.

Inland Waterways Association, PO Box 114, Rickmansworth, Hertfordshire WD3 1ZY. Tel: (01923) 711114.
www.waterways.org.uk
E-mail: iwa@waterways.org.uk

Living Streets, 31–33 Bondway, Vauxhall London SW8
1SJ. Tel: (020) 7820 1010.
www.livingstreets.org.uk

Mother Earth, www.motherearth.org

National Trust, Rowan House, Kembrey Park, Swindon,
Wiltshire SN2 6UG. Tel: (01793) 462800.
www.nationaltrust.org.uk

Sustrans Limited, 35 King Street, Bristol BS1 4DZ. Tel: (0117) 926 8893. www.sustrans.org.uk
E-mail: info@sustrans.org.uk Promoting sustainable transport.

Waterway Recovery Group, PO Box 114, Rickmansworth, Hertfordshire WD3 1ZY. Tel: (01923) 711114. www.wrg.org.uk

Index